Published by WEBB RESEARCH GROUP
Direct all inquiries to the distributor:
PACIFIC NORTHWEST BOOKS COMPANY
(SAN 200-5263)
P.O. Box 314 Medford, Oregon 97501

Library of Congress Cataloging in Publication Data

Webber, Bert.
  Oregon covered bridges : an Oregon documentary in pictures / Bert
and Margie Webber ; photographs by John Snook and others.
    p.   cm.
  Includes bibliographical references and index.
  ISBN 0-936738-65-0 (limited ed.) : $24.95. — ISBN 0-936738-56-1
(pbk) : $14.95
  1. Covered bridges—Oregon. I. Webber, Margie. II. Snook, John,
1918-   .   III. Webb Research Group. IV. Title.
TG24.07W43 1991
624´.37´09795—dc20   90-13064
                                                CIP   Rev.

Contents

(Next Page) Goodpasture covered bridge.
McKenzie River May 1983. "Ten minutes
later it rained — buckets — and the bridge
was glad it had its hat on."
Glenn Barkhurst.

Fred Kildow

Fred Kildow, a native Oregonian, is acknowledged by "bridgers" nationwide as the Dean of Oregon covered bridges.

Fred was one of the founders of the Covered Bridge Society of Oregon in 1978 and was the society's first president (1979-1981). He was later corresponding secretary for many years and his address has been used as a stability point for the organization for years "as other come and go."

Kildow has been interested in covered bridges since the 1930's when he drove through some in his Model T Ford. He became seriously interested in them in 1971 when he noticed a sign that had been tacked to the wall of Lost Creek covered bridge in Jackson County. The little poster had been put there by a visitor from the Northern Ohio covered bridge society.

When Fred was on a trip in Ohio in 1972, he and his party stopped a road repair crew and asked if there happened to be a covered bridge nearby. The men gave directions not to just one but to three. On seeing them, Fred immediately adopted covered bridges as his No. 1 hobby.

In 1945 he married Mary DiSanto. He and Mary parented and enjoy four children (1 boy and 3 girls) and presently have five grandchildren. They live in a southwest suburb of Portland where their home is appropriately decorated with every type of artwork relating to covered bridges.

It is with pride that we dedicate this book to
Fred Kildow
Dean of Oregon Covered Bridges
Webb Research Group, Publishers

Covered Bridges all around us

One might squint his eyes to look across a pasture and in his mind's eye see a pair of boys trudging along toward a creek. These boys, each carrying home-made fishing poles, were headed for the old covered bridge that spanned the creek at the deepest of nearby fishing holes. On the far side of the creek were very old fir trees with a mix of cedar. The trees cast a deep shadow on the fishing hole. This was good for fishing.

Many years of horse-drawn wagons had clopped and rolled across this bridge and time had taken its toll. The creek could be seen through patched floorboards while sunlight finds its way through vacancies in the roof.

Intent on their destination, these anglers cared very little that ''old people'' were more likely to associate these quaint structures with New England than with the far west. And they might be surprised to learn that the first covered bridge built west of the Mississippi River was erected by a New Englander. The builder, John T. Little, built an ambitious structure that stretched 550 feet across the waters of the South Fork of the American River at Salmon Falls in California. This was in 1850.

In Oregon, the first covered bridge was recorded a year later in Oregon City when a four year old open-top bridge was roofed. While a 405 foot long timber truss across the North Fork of the Yamhill River in Lafayette was started in 1850, its completion was delayed until 1852 because of flooding. Ironically, both bridges were lost with the next high water during the flood of 1853. Pioneer bridge-builders had not yet learned how to deal with the fickle waters of the west. Being neither architects nor engineers, they often built covered bridges too close to the waters they spanned. Unfortunately many of these early structures did not survive. Fortunately for the bridge buff of today, Oregon's often soggy weather and high rivers did not deter these builders. During the decades that followed, covered bridges would represent some of the best bridges ever built.

*   *   *

History of covered bridges reaches far back in time. The *World Guide To Covered Bridges* (1989 edition) lists the bridge longest standing as being in a Liechtenstein courtyard over a mountain stream. It was built in 1135.

The old London Bridge is described in this prose:

...the tide flowed under the narrow archways like a mill-race on this bridge which was completed in 1209 and survived with its tunnel-like street of shops and houses for more than 600 years. *-The Encyclopedia Britannica* (1971)

In Persia, bridges such as the Allah Verdi Kahn and the Pul Khajoo, were designed as cool, shaded retreats where travelers could find rooms for rest and refreshments after crossing hot desert sands. The two-storied Pul Khajoo, at Isfahan, which took from 1647 to 1667 to complete, had 24 pointed arches that carried an 85-foot wide roadway. There were walled passages above it along the top of a dam.

Swiss carpenters Hans and Johannes Grubenmann built covered timber bridges with spans up to 193-feet long at Schaffhausen, over the Rhine River, during 1756-1758. Their greatest triumph was their 240-foot span at Reichenan.

In the United States, the first timber truss was over the Connecticut River at Bellows Falls, Vermont built by Enoch Hale in 1795.

The "Colossus" Bridge was a 340-foot covered span at Fairmont, Pennsylvania over the Schuykill River built in 1812.

The 360-foot long record-breaker for span length was the McCall's Ferry Bridge erected in 1815 by Theodore Burr. He used his own design, the Burr Truss, which set a pattern for covered bridges made of wood in America. These early covered bridges have gone their way with the oldest in the country at the present time at Glimmerglass State Park in Ostego County, New York where it crosses Shadow Brook. This is a 53-foot Burr truss built in 1823.

While the golden era of bridge building in America was between 1800 and 1900, we noted Oregon's first covered bridge was in 1851.

Of the covered bridges known to be standing in Oregon at the present time, state records and research by bridge buffs suggest the oldest to be Drift Creek bridge in Lincoln County (1914). But one must be careful about dates of origin because longtime residents are persistently loud in their statements that some bridges are much older. When reading early newspaper accounts of accidents on the bridges, as well as other events, the construction dates frequently creep in. We will run into some of these in this book.

Some writers report Oregon has had as many as 500 covered bridges since 1851. Although we searched diligently to document such a number, we could come up with only 286. These appear on a 1948 list of the former Oregon State Highway Department's Traffic Engineering Division, compiled from the "Index of Covered Bridges in Oregon-1947." It is not possible to determine the earliest due to two factors:

1. On that list, 119 spans are shown "date unknown" as to when built.

Tacoma, Washington   June 6, 1988

I was born in Lake Creek, Jackson County in 1911 and I can't remember of the Lost Creek covered bridge not being there. My father worked in the mine on Lost Creek and we visited friends at the mine and I can remember the bridge was there at that time. We left in February 1919 and the covered bridge was there before we left.*

Mrs. Clara Michi Munt

---

* The Southern Oregon Historical Society assertively declares the Lost Creek covered bridge was built in 1919. For additonal data, see entry for Lost Creek covered bridge.

Laurelhurst covered bridge was replaced by Peyton concrete bridge in 1961. Then Peyton bridge was covered up by Lost Creek Lake in a Rogue River flood control project in the 1980's. The present steel girder bridge on highway 62 over Lost Creek is nearly directly above the old bridge sites. The earlier covered bridge was also called the Peyton-Laurelhurst bridge.

An historic covered bridge is part of the design for this U.S. postage stamp issued in 1952 marking the Centennial of Engineering.

2. This list is gross in its error of omission. Cite: Jackson County records reveal that the Hartman brothers built or worked on 27 covered bridges in the county. In an article in the Medford *Mail Tribune* (July 19, 1954), the brothers named 8 bridges standing at that time. The 1947 state list shows only 5.

Of the covered bridges standing today, most were built between 1910 and 1950. Reported by decades we discover:

1910-1919	6	1950-1959	1
1920-1929	18	1960-1969	2
1930-1939	16	1970-1979	-
1940-1949	5	1980-1989	4
		1990-	1

The West has been known for its use of the superlative and can lay claim to the newest, tallest, longest, widest, most northerly, closest to the water covered bridges. But, as we have seen, the West cannot claim the earliest.

It seems wise to look at the guidelines some folks use to define a covered bridge.

To start with, for a covered bridge to be "traditional," it should be supported by a wood truss. The bridge should be made mostly of wood, at least that part from the deck (roadway) up — but there may be metal tension rods in the truss. While traditionalists also want wooden sides and a wood roof, there are many examples of corregated iron, or flat sheet-metal roofs as well as metal sides. Of course a covered bridge should have a roof but there are exceptions. As the base plan for a covered bridge is the truss, some truss bridges were completed without the traditional roof. Examples are some railroad bridges in Washington state where bridge engineers apparently wanted to protect their structures against flying cinders from puffing locomotives — left the roof off.

Some covered bridges over the years have lost their tops due to fires — which seem to have been the major threat — but the truss and deck have remained in service. Other qualifications include that the bridge, when built, was supposed to have been for vehicles, the decks eight or more feet wide. Further, the bridge must serve a worthwhile purpose as crossing a stream of any size, a gulch through which seasonal runoff occurred, a ravine or a railroad. While some golfing clubs are said to be building "quaint little covered bridges for use by golf carts," none of these are included here.

This book is intended as a reference guide and for enjoyment thus we do not quibble if the bridge is on public or private ground or if something about the construction does not meet the purest test as to what materials might have been used or how it was put together. Time changes

In 1922, Wesley and Lyal Hartman, bridge builders and fixers in Jackson County, set out in one of the two 1919 Model T Ford trucks the county owned, for a bridge site in the wilderness. The first job was to establish camp, where they would live for several weeks until the bridge was finished. They carried rifles for protection from bears, as well as to provide fresh meat for their table. Time flies, when you're having fun. The boys liked their work which was often 12 to 14 hours a day.

Teams of horses were hired by the day to pound bridge pilings into the ground. The team would lift a weight on the end of a long rope, the rope run through a pully atop a tall frame. On signal, the weight would be released and would fall, hitting the pole (piling) driving it into the ground. Bridge building was not known to be speedy.

Long timbers, chords in bridge language, on trailer being readied to be pulled to a construction site in 1925. (Lower) Lyal and Wesley Hartman with wheel-wrench which was used, by up to five men, to tighten tension on metal rods on Howe trusses.

Many early covered bridges had limited clearance and it was common for high-profile log trucks to sweep through the bridge and crash the ends. Finally, bridge crews raised and squared off many portals, put a transom in one that was opened for high loads by pulling a rope, and designed Cavitt covered bridge with a high arch. Our picture of a loaded log truck, for illustration, is contemporary and is considerably lower profile than usually seen in earlier years.

many things. Today a covered bridge's foundation does not often come into argument be it made of pilings hammered into the muck with the use of a team of horses, or poured cement, or pre-stressed concrete piers dropped into place with a diesel-powered crane.

Our fisherboys probably never considered that some of those huge trees not all that far from the bridge may have been felled just to build this bridge. Anyway, if the trees had been used for such a proud thing as a covered bridge, that should be all right. As a renewable resource, new trees would take their place. Early builders chose sites for some of their bridges close to tall trees. This eliminated hauling. Western red cedar was abundant in western Oregon and it was not a choice for general dimension lumber in those days. Much of it was used in covered bridges.

Douglas fir was the overwhelming favorite. The trees grew thick and many were very tall. The tall trees were ideal for use in bridges over wide waterways. There is a reddish hue to these woods which led oldtimers to quip that the bridges were "rusted from all the rain." Fir gripped nails more firmly than other species and inhibited the corrosion of the metal parts set in it. These trees were often called "Paul Bunyon's Toothpicks" because of their length and straightness.

It took a lot of work to prepare timbers then build a bridge and builders, be they private businessmen, or a county court, sought ways to recover the costs — tolls. Oregon Provisional Government Act of December 17, 1845 established a minimum for toll rates. This is interesting as an economic index.

Single horse and carriage	18ᶜ
Man and horse	10ᶜ
Horses and cattle per head	3ᶜ

An 1887 order decreed that persons going to funerals, to church services or to vote in a public election would be exempt from paying tolls. Tradition has it that "widow women" were also allowed to pass over the covered bridge free of toll.

It has traditionally been something of a game to try to beat the toll-taker of his fees. Youngsters, and some oldsters as well, often hid under a load of hay (much like kids of a later generation hiding in the trunks of cars as a way to sneak into drive-in movies). Some of the early free-thinkers considered the entire toll requirement as government trying to force them to use the bridge — forded the streams. Tollgate keepers had to allow those who wanted to wade do so as the law was clear that only those who used the bridge paid.

Occasionally the job of toll-taker was dangerous. In 1857, George Irwin, who seems to have been known as "quarrelsome-George," was the owner of the Pudding River Toll Bridge in Clackamas County. One day he fired upon a Mr. Martindale who had failed to meet the toll requirements. George missed but Martindale, in return fire did not. George might have been right in demanding toll, but now he was *dead right*.

Later, Martindale was tried and found not guilty on the grounds of self-defense. This is said to have furthered the demand for toll-free bridges. Today, one can cross any of the remaining covered bridges on Oregon's public road toll-free. The only remaining toll, treasured by romantics, is the age-old ritual of stealing a kiss from a sweetheart when passing through the portals of these bridges.

Covered bridges have been jocularly called by various names of which here are a few: flying barns, floating boxes, roofs over rivers, kissing bridges, haunted bridges and dog houses large enough to comfortably house Elmer, Paul Bunyon's hunting dog.

Covered bridges have served as temporary shelter for families in need. Many a bootlegging transaction sought concealment within a covered bridge. The bridges served as hangouts for hooligans, pranksters, a place where youngsters could hide to puff an illicit cigarette. The bridges have been sanctuaries for wildlife — and bugs — and for lovers. And a number of robberies have taken place in them, too.

During periods of strife they served as rallying points for the militia.

Rows of mail boxes have been sheltered within covered bridges but we have not found that a post office ever operated from inside a covered bridge.

The questions come up sooner or later, "Why are covered bridges covered?"

In 1862, a tongue-in-cheek editor of an Oregon paper wrote:

> Though the builders do not feel ashamed of their
> work, they are busily engaged in covering it up.

But those of a more practical inclination suggested that old bridges could be recycled as barns when they were worn out and no longer needed for crossing a river. It was also suggested that in years of abundant production of hay, the extra crop might be stored in the peaks of the covered bridges.

While the majority of covered bridges in Oregon are easily seen and are painted white, others might be missed in the wink-of-an-eye as one speeds along a road. Rock O' The Range in Deschutes County is one that is easily missed.

Covered bridge art
Flower bowl (Artist not identified)

The authors appreciate the assistance given by the various artists whose works appear in this book. It must be pointed out that black and white photographs are only a poor substitute for viewing the fine originals.

Some thought the roofs were to foil the cattle, that sometimes had to be aggressively forced to cross a bridge, by letting the cow think she was entering her barn!

The truth is much more mundane. There appear to be three primary reasons to put a lid on a bridge:

1. An unhoused structure was subject to spring and winter rains and snow and, in time, deteriorated. It was considered no longer safe after ten years. A roof provided runoff for the wet and extended the life of the bridge by at least three fold
2. Sides and roof on a bridge gave added strength to the entire structure — skin tension
3. Adding sides and roofs to bridges gave needed business to lumber mills suffering from the doldrums which from time-to-time plagued the timber industry.

The latter was a suggestion of Oregon's deputy state engineer, Mr. Contine.

In 1932, his successor, C.B. McCullough, offered the same suggestion this time to alleviate the then glut of northwest lumber idle in the yards. Currently, one might add:

4. Covered bridges are considered "folk architecture" and are attractions for tourists

5. The ailing timber industry would be aided if more covered bridges were built then means sought to encourage spotted owls to nest in the rafters.

*   *   *

No discussion about covered bridges can be complete without some understanding of the word, "truss." As a verb, "truss" indicates what a chef does to a chicken or turkey before roasting it. As a noun, "truss" is a scientific contribution of the Renaissance. Andrea Palladio, a 16th Century architect, is credited with designing an arrangement of a rigid triangle in wood — the truss. Palladio put together what we now call "kingpost" and "queenpost" truss bridges.

The kingpost is the simplest design. It consists of a center post framed into two triangles by a bottom chord. A major drawback to the kingpost is that for a very heavy load, longer (higher) diagonals must be used. Since Paul Bunyon's Toothpicks were not widely available, the solution was to maintain a low profile by adding more diagonals but in so doing the centers had no support thus, the queen post was the answer. This was a "stretched" version of two kingposts joined together with a horizontal rail or "chord." At this writing, the single remaining kingpost in Oregon is Neal Lane Covered Bridge in Douglas County.

Covered bridge art
Potholder (Edna Erdmann)

Common Truss Designs in Oregon.

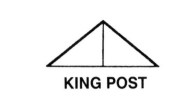

KING POST

(WOOD)
TRADITIONAL TRUSS
ORIGIN IN THE MIDDLE AGES

LENGTH 20-60 FEET
(6-18 METERS)

QUEEN POST

(WOOD)
LENGTHENED VERSION OF THE
KING POST

LENGTH 20-80 FEET
(6-24 METERS)

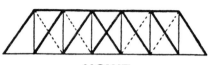

HOWE

(WOOD, VERTICALS OF METAL)
DIAGONALS IN COMPRESSION,
VERTICALS IN TENSION

LENGTH 30-150 FEET
(9-45 METERS)

There are five queenpost covered bridges presently standing:

1. Lost Creek Covered Bridge - Jackson County
2. Antelope Creek Covered Bridge - Jackson County (recently moved to Little Butte Creek and renamed Eagle Point Covered Bridge
3. Wimer Covered Bridge - Jackson County
4. North Fork Covered Bridge - Lincoln County
5. Fourtner Covered Bridge - Polk County

Nearly all remaining covered bridges in Oregon are Howe trusses. William Howe developed his truss in 1840. It is a modification of the kingpost using metal rods (tension bolts) which give added support. These rods are threaded. This allows for adjusting the tension at critical truss joints and prevents sagging.

Robert W. Smith introduced his Smith Truss in 1867. This was also called a "half-lattice" as it featured a series of diagonal struts resembling a row of **XXXXX** secured to the top and lower cords. Although the Smith at one time dominated covered bridge design, there are no standing examples in Oregon today.

In the 1988 study by the Oregon Department of Transportation, prepared as a report for the 1989 legislature, two other trusses are mentioned.

1. Steel girder — Milo Academy Covered Bridge, Douglas County
2. Deck girder — Rock O' the Range Covered Bridge, Deschutes County; Cedar Crossing Bridge, Multnomah County

An ingenuous, "pre-fabricated" girder has recently made its appearance and thus far has not appeared in any state report. What to do with old railroad flat cars that the railroads love to sell? We find one as the base for a covered bridge in Lake County and — the newest covered bridge in Oregon — in the middle of the City of Arlington in Gilliam County.

The city of Cottage Grove is billed as "The Covered Bridge Capital of Oregon." It is in Lane County, that county claiming more covered bridges standing than any other coun-

Models of trusses used in classroom by Orville Erdmann. (Top) King, Smith (Lower) Howe, Queen

Covered Bridge art
Decorated circular saw blade (A. Lee)

ty, one fellow claiming there are more covered bridges within a 50 mile radius than any similar area on earth. Oregon is sixth in the U.S.A. for number of standing covered bridges but where else can one point to such majestically tall and straight trees.

What lies ahead for these charming examples of "folk" architecture? Is the value merely local interest or of state and national importance? Many of these bridges qualify for listing in the *National Register of Historic Places*. Some communities have set up local-interest groups and there is the Covered Bridge Society of Oregon — the only such organization in the western United States. The society is dedicated to the preservation and restoration of Oregon covered bridges. Membership is open to the public. The Society publishes a regular newsletter for members.

The National Society for the Preservation of Covered Bridges seeks to generate interest in covered bridges and provides meetings and services to bridge buffs. This society brings out a newsletter as well as a quarterly magazine both being sent to the membership, which is open to all who are interested in covered bridges.

Joseph Conwill, writing in the present edition of *World Guide to Covered Bridges* (1989 edition) discusses "Covered Bridge Preservation":

26

Why preserve covered bridges: For nostalgia? Perhaps in part, but also for progress. It is not progress to destroy the past for then we learn nothing. Rather, it is progress to build on the past. The preservation of covered bridges is part of the preservation of historic places in general which is necessary that we may not forget who we are.

In Jackson County there have been three major covered bridge reclamations recently completed. These are the Antelope Creek bridge moved into the city of Eagle Point where it was installed over Little Butte Creek; the McKee bridge, near Ruch; and the Lost Creek covered bridge rebuilding project completed in late 1990. Local societies spearheaded each of these projects with many fund-raisers as well as limited public money. There have been other such projects throughout Oregon. In Albany, a boosters organization is said to have advertised that any covered bridge declared surplus, or to be replaced by highway modernization, or any other plan, let the folks there know for they are interested in removing the bridge and setting it up at Albany.

Where practical, the State suggests that when a covered bridge has lost its effectiveness due to highway improvements, these should be left standing and "bypassed" and a rest area might be located there. It is plausible that road or park funds might be available for developing the rest areas.

Covered bridge art
Untitled (Mary Jane)

A comprehensive study for use by the State Legislature was developed for restoring and maintaining covered bridges in Oregon. The study concludes that such a project is worthwhile and possible. In some instances money may be available from Oregon Department of Transportation's highway fund, Parks and Recreation Department, Grants-in-Aid, state lottery proceeds, Federal Historic Preservation funds and in some cases, the plausibility of tax credits.

Covered bridges in Oregon have already become an important part in the statewide tourist-attracting program. Research completed at Oregon State University cites that while covered bridges are not usually a "final destination" attraction, the numbers of people interested in covered bridges is significant and contributes positively to the overall tourist effort in the state. Listed as the second most important reason for visiting Oregon were visits to historical and cultural sites. These include covered bridges.

Accordingly, there are efforts in every county in which there are covered bridges, and in the towns and cities nearest to the bridges, to take care of them. No longer can a county roadmaster decide that an old covered bridge is not serviceable and send his crew out to tear it down. This has happened in the past but the probability of it ever occurring again is almost nil. When the word gets out that a certain bridge

Covered Bridge art
Rural mail box (Geannie Newell)

Covered bridge art
Pine needle and raffia hanging (Lorene Mathews)

is in "difficulty," concerned citizens get together, promote the preservation of *their* bridge, raise the money to fix it. At the present time there are funds in highway department coffers for assistance, and often matching money from the state lottery under the economic development (tourism) classification. Although some state money may be available for such projects, these funds are only contributing in nature and become available after much work, meetings, rummage sales and the like at the local level.

Of very significant assistance is the willingness of major contractors, those firms owning huge cranes, 30-wheel flatbed trucks, king-size bulldozers and the like, to loan the equipment, and the drivers — sometimes entire crews — to these projects. We could never name them all here. In Jackson County there was the dismantling, moving and setting up of Antelope Creek covered bridge several miles away in Eagle Point where it now rests over Little Butte Creek. There was the pick-it-up—fix-it—set-it-back-down work on Lost Creek covered bridge. Pacific Power and Light Company, and the various telephone companies, are frequently involved because of the need to move overhead wires, traffic signals and the like while a bridge passes underneath on a flatbed truck or on house-moving dollies. Such efforts bring out law enforcement agencies to direct traffic during the work which

Covered bridge art
Larwood bridge (Bev Jungwirth)

includes crowd control. Just about everybody turns out, along with TV crews, to be awed at the sight of a 120-foot long skeleton moving slowly along the road. When all the chores are finished and the grand opening takes place, such events are celebrated with 4th-of-July enthusiasm.

While covered bridges no longer need to serve as havens for dislocated families or hangouts for bootleggers, they still provide a place for fisherboys, pranksters and, of course, lovers.

It was said that old toll collectors hung a line under their bridge to let their laundry dangle-splash in the river allowing the current to do the washing.

The bridge tenders are gone and with them their wash lines, but covered bridges in Oregon are here to stay.

* * *

The authors are indebted to many fine people who contributed to this research and writing project. Frederick Kildow, dean of Oregon covered bridge enthusiasts, entertained our inquiries many times. We came away from every visit more knowledgeable, having had the help of this friendly gentleman. We recognize his authority and dedicate this book to Fred.

Steve Webber, Archivist of the City of Portland, a nephew, searched for early covered bridge material and rewarded us with much data. He was on our trek to Widing, lost-among-the-blackberries covered bridge the day we visited it and made the photos appearing here. Steve is an enthusiastic archivist and we appreciate his input.

Orville Erdmann, of Bandon, teaches a class on history of Oregon covered bridges at Southwestern Oregon Community College at Coos Bay. He arranged his schedule for a visit from us then shared his notes and picture collection. We are thankful for his help.

Ben Dahlenburg, Sweethome, responded enthusiastically when we requested details about his high school building trades class that builds covered bridges as well as houses. Fred's bridge projects, three of them, are detailed here. We appreciate his interest in this project and his assistance.

About the newest covered bridge in Oregon, China Ditch in Arlington, Kay West accepted our probing inquiries, provided useful information and suggested additional sources including Steve Seed also of Arlington. We reached Bob Pepperling on his ranch in Canada who described his flatcar-base covered bridge in Lake County. Walt Leeuwenburgh, Jackson County Public Works Road Department, welcomed us and gladly answered questions then provided his file on the county's covered bridges for our use. Numerous folks in the Oregon Department of Transportation walked us through the

Covered bridge art
Gilkey bridge / upper; Grave Creek bridge / lower
(Evelyn Bennett)

Covered bridge art
Museum model in glass case (Orville Erdmann)

maze of data, helped us gather information and allowed us to microfilm selected portions of this, especially historical photographs, for our book. Morris X. Smith, the grand senior gentleman who has lived within an arm's reach of Chitwood covered bridge nearly all his life, willingly shared the history of the bridge, much of which we did not earlier know to ask. He quipped that the recently rebuilt bridge "will outlast all of us." And it was Morris, on learning that the Elk City covered bridge had plunged into the Yaquina River, roared 7 miles over there with his Olympus OM camera, recorded the scene then loaned the picture for use here. Jerry Winterbotham, who is a published historian about the Elkton area, mentioned to us that he had pictures of two very early covered bridges in that area. We are pleased to reproduce Jerry's pictures here. We could go on as there were others who came to our attention during the course of this work but names blur in the excitement of trying to get it all together. To all those mentioned, as well as those not, we truly appreciate your input.

We were fortunate in meeting John Snook. He spent the first ten of his retirement years making the rounds of all standing Oregon covered bridges and photographed them. His previously unpublished pictures appear here, with much thanks, for a book of this nature requires quality photographs.

Covered bridge art
Punch needle wall hanging (Greta Forbish)

Pictures by others have been added where needed.

Of significance in all of our writing projects is that we recognize the need for professional library research. Of great professional help and friendliness is the staff at Jackson County Library System's Medford Main Branch. Anne Billeter, Ph.D., heads the Reference Department. The present staff librarians are Larry Calkins, Jan Gorden, Sheila Hungerford, Kate McGann, Maureen Schroeder, Scott Wootten, Amy Kinard and Judy Kennedy. We thank them all.

We are also mindful that in spite of care, some omissions or errors may be noted. Should this be true, constructive criticism is invited to the attention of the publisher.

Bert and Margie Webber
Central Point, Oregon
Winter 1990-91

Gilkey covered bridge in 1984 (left) and in 1990 (lower).

Name: **Belknap** *World Guide* No. 37-20-11
Linn County
Type/Year: Howe 1966
Length: 120 feet 1 span
Spans: McKenzie River
Nearest Town: McKenzie Bridge
Remarks:

Named for early pioneers, Belknap Bridge is in good condition with no immediate repairs indicated. Used by local traffic and log hauling trucks up to 35 tons. Also known as "McKenzie River Bridge," it replaces three earlier covered bridges that were built in 1890, 1911, 1938. The bridge was modified in 1975 by adding windows on the south side for illumination. Here is one of the few covered bridges in Oregon that regularly gets a covering of snow. The bridge is in the Deschutes National Forest.

Located off highway 126 on McKenzie River Drive near site of old village/post office of Rainbow.

Name: Bohemian Hall   *World Guide* No. 37-22-07
Linn County
Type/Year: Howe 1947
Length: 120 feet 1 span
Spans: Crabtree Creek (moved — in storage)
Nearest Town: Scio
Remarks:

This covered bridge got its name from Czechoslovakian settlers who began a community in the vicinity of the bridge — the name from the Tolstoj ZCBJ Lodge — about 1922. The bridge replaced an earlier span on the Richardson Gap site. It had been known as the Richardson Gap covered bridge, that name from the family, Richardson, that had a spread there in the 1880's. The bridge was replaced with a concrete span in 1987 but was taken down piece-by-piece. The top and sides were sheet metal and came off easily. Enthused by the restorations of other covered bridges, a group in Albany plans to relocate Bohemian Hall covered bridge to the Timber-Linn Park on Price Road in Albany. The enthusiasm for the project is very great and at this writing plans are firming but no date has been set. State lottery money has been requested. In the meantime, one can get an excellent view of the skeleton of a genuine covered bridge with all its wraps off — a most unique scene — by going to the county maintenance shop and yard near Scio where the entire Howe truss is parked in the rear of the yard at the corner of Richardson Gap Road and highway 226.

For directions, see how to get to Shimanek covered bridge. The gate to the property may be locked on weekends.

When there was talk about tearing down the old Antelope Creek covered bridge the folks in and around the town of Eagle Point rushed to rescue the bridge. Today, moved and rebuilt, the bridge is now known as Eagle Point covered bridge. See pages 54-57.

Name: **Cavitt** *World Guide* No. 37-10-06
Douglas County
Type/Year: Howe 1943
Length: 70 feet 1 span
Spans: Little River at Confluence with Cavitt Creek
Nearest Town: Glide
Remarks:

Named for Robert Cavitt, an early settler. Unique, as it has asphalt laid over the wood deck, metal siding. Used by local traffic with 3-ton limit. The high, arched portals were designed to accommodate high loads on log trucks. Cavitt Bridge is in good condition.

On Cavitt Creek Road at intersection of county roads 17 and 82.

Name: **Cedar Crossing** *World Guide* No. 37-26-X2
Multnomah County
Type/Year: Deck Girder (Glulam stringer) 1982
Length: 60 feet 1 span
Spans: Johnson Creek
Nearest Town: Portland at 134th St. and Deardorf Road
Remarks:

Cedar Crossing is considered by just about everybody as a "covered bridge" because it is a bridge with a roof. However, purists call it a "roofed span" because it lacks traditional wood trusses. The bridge replaces, at cost of $168,250, an older uncovered span that was removed in November 1981 because it was too narrow to accommodate increased traffic. Interior of knotty pine — is lighted at night. New bridge has 5-foot wide sidewalk separated from road by guard rail — is only pedestrian and vehicle crossing of Johnson Creek for some distance.

From Interstate-5 take Foster Road exit east to 134th Street then south to sharp turn to east and down steep, narrow grade on Deardorf Road into gully. Sharp, low-speed curves.

Name: Centennial *World Guide* No. 37-20-41
Lane County
Type/Year: Howe 1987
Length: 84 feet 1 span
Spans: Coast Fork Willamette River
Nearest Town: Cottage Grove
Remarks:

This covered bridge received its name because it was built for and dedicated on the centennial of Cottage Grove in June 1987. Trusses in the bridge came from two older covered bridges that had been dismantled and stored for some bright day when they might be reused. The trusses were from Meadows covered bridge near Mapleton and from Brumbaugh covered bridge near Cottage Grove. Centennial covered bridge is a model, at 3/8-inch scale, of Chambers covered bridge. (Chambers is a derelict extra-tall railroad bridge that still stands in Cottage Grove down the street a few blocks.) A story in the Cottage Grove *Sentinel* reported that Lane County moved the trusses from its storage yard to a local sawmill where the timbers were cut for the new project, then the tension rod-bolts were adapted and re-threaded to fit. The paper continued that many volunteers donated their Saturday time to work on the bridge. After finishing the work and during the dedication, a time-capsule was inserted in the bridge. The new bridge, intended just for pedestrians, is lighted for night use. It is only 10-feet wide and parallels an older concrete span for vehicles.

The bridge is on Main Street on the west side of the original downtown area. In summer, all the window boxes on the bridge are abloom with flowers. The bridge is very photogenic from many angles.

Name: **Chambers** *World Guide* No. 37-20-40
Lane County
Type/Year: Howe 1936
Length: 78 feet 1 span
Spans: Coast Fork Willamette River
Nearest Town: Cottage Grove
Remarks:

Named for Frank Chambers Mill in Cottage Grove, the bridge was built for trains hauling logs to the mill hence the very tall, ungainly appearance. When new, the sides were completely covered but now the trusses are exposed revealing very high-angled trusses and multi-use of triple tension rods needed to support heavily loaded trains which ceased after the mill burned in 1943. Only covered bridge of its type, privately owned and abandoned. Is perched high enough to dissuade most people from crawling on it but dangerous for those who do. Condition very poor with the extreme weight causing beginning of collapse on one corner. Estimate of $80,000 for needed repairs with no present plans to fix it. Very photogenic due to unusual shape.

Go on South River Road some blocks south of Centennial Bridge.

Chambers covered bridge as viewed from the south (above) and from inside looking west (far right). Climbing on this bridge is not recommended. Note three tension rods (inset) for Howe truss. Pictures on page 41: End view from east of the river facing west. Inset, closeup of deterioration is on right corner of the bridge when facing the bridge from the street.

Name: **China Ditch**
World Guide No. 37-11-X1
Gilliam County
Type/Year: RR flat car 1990
Length: 67 feet 1 span
Spans: China Ditch
Nearest Town: Arlington
Remarks:

The City of Arlington and China Ditch, a spring run-off drain from nearby hills, is at the mouth of Alkali Canyon at the Columbia River. A consortium of several businesses in town decided that a covered bridge over the drainage ditch would be appropriate, so set about doing it. For a suitable deck, the committee decided on an 85-foot long railroad flat car. The car was cut to 67-feet long needed for their covered bridge. This was a community project but the land and bridge are owned by the City of Arlington. The bridge is 10-feet wide (inside measurement) and could accommodate automobiles, but the project is intended only for pedestrians. Steve Seed, of the Chemical Waste Management Company, one of the firms in the group, was site manager. The Big River Band Festival committee maintains the covered bridge and holds an annual celebration each June. A dedication and announcement of the winning formal name for the bridge is planned for June 15, 1991.

The covered bridge can be seen from the eastbound lanes of I-84. Arlington, a major exit off I-84, is 153 miles east of Portland.

Name: **Chitwood**   *World Guide* No. 37-21-03
Lincoln County
Type/Year: Howe 1926 (rebuilt 1984)
Length: 96 feet 1 span
Spans: Yaquina River
Nearest Town: Eddyville
Remarks:

Citizens of Lincoln County love their covered bridges and when Chitwood became dilapidated, strong sentiment led to its preservation and restoration at a bill of $244,000. Once a small logging and railroad siding community where there had been a post office from 1887 to 1945, Chitwood is now a tiny rural settlement with few remaining residents including Morris X. Smith, son of earlier general store proprietor and postmaster.

On highway 20 west of Eddyville — watch for it or you will speed right past it!

44

(Facing page) Chitwood covered bridge today and during reconsruction showing temporary bypass on right. (This page) Morris X. Smith who has lived at the site most of his life, at corner of once-proud general store and post office, near the bridge. Old bridge and diving board with skiff of snow. (Left) New bridge on a very rainy day — note "line" of rain in river and "still" water under the bridge.

Name: **Coyote Creek** *World Guide* No. 37-20-02
Lane County
Type/Year: Howe 1922
Length: 60 feet 1 span
Spans: Coyote Creek
Nearest Town: Hadleyville
Remarks:

    Earlier known as "Battle Creek Bridge" and "Swing Log Bridge." This covered bridge is in good shape after having the roof replaced in early 1970. (The roof had collapsed under about 3-feet of snow — "unusual weather" say locals.) It is on an early Territorial Road that was incorporated into the state highway system.

    Off highway 126, west of Eugene on Battle Creek Road near site of Hadleyville.

Name: **Crawfordsville**   *World Guide* No. 37-22-15
Linn County
Type/Year: Howe   1932
Length: 105 feet   1 span
Spans: Calapooia River
Nearest Town: Crawfordsville
Remarks:

Named for Philemon Crawford, who founded the town and whose son was the postmaster. The covered bridge had rounded entry-ways until the highway department enlarged and braced the corners to handle bigger loads. The bridge became the focal point of a county park when it was bypassed in 1963 in a highway redesign project. In 1976 the bridge was painted and was featured in the TV movie "The Flood." It has been kept up by residents including a major brush clearing festival by volunteers of the Covered Bridge Society of Oregon in 1986. A Federal program putting unemployed persons to work renovated the bridge in 1987 as a project of Community Services Consortium at a cost of $23,000. Crawfordsville covered bridge is in good condition.

Highway 228 to Crawfordsville via Brownsville.

Name: **Currin** *World Guide* No. 37-20-22

Lane County

Type/Year: Howe 1925

Length: 105 feet 1 span

Spans: Row River

Nearest Town: Cottage Grove

Remarks:

The first bridge here was built in 1883 and was replaced by county workers at a cost of nearly $2,500 less than a contractor's bid in 1925. It was bypassed in 1979, when new concrete span was built just a few feet away. Although the approach closest to the main highway has been removed (Row River Road), pedestrian access is available from the other end of the bridge by crossing on the concrete span to the other side. Condition is poor — not presently funded for repairs.

Take Row River Road from town.

Name: **Dahlenburg** *World Guide* No. 37-22-X1
Linn County
Type/Year: Howe 1989
Length: 20 feet 1 span
Spans: Ames Creek
Nearest Town: Sweethome
Remarks:

Dahlenburg covered bridge is named in honor of school teacher, Ben Dahlenburg, Sweethome High School, whose Building Trades class designed and built the bridge as a class project for which each sudent received a report card grade. The on-the-job training class wanted to build a house but property wasn't then available so they decided to build a covered bridge. Using a model on exhibit in the public library and many library books about covered bridges, the class designed a bridge then scaled it in chalk on the floor of the school shop. From this a blueprint was developed then with city funds, $2,000, the boys built the bridge. This is a Howe truss bridge with the heaviest timbers being 4 x 8-inch and 4 x 6-inch. The 20-foot bridge is 12-feet wide. It is mounted across Ames Creek, near Weddle Bridge, which this class also substantially rebuilt. Dahlenberg covered bridge is used by walkers only.

An additional project, a "portable" covered bridge, was built by the class then mounted on a donated mobile home chassis. This unit is 8-feet wide and 20-feet long. The purpose of the trailer is to promote covered bridge preservation by being seen in parades and civic events of nearby cities. While the trailer-bridge was on exhibit in Sankey Park one day, a man from New England — that area also noted for a number of covered bridges — saw the little portable bridge and learned it had been built in a school shop as a class project. He declared he'd like to buy it. He was told the price. In a few days his check was received with a note indicating maybe someday he'd come to get it but probably not. Indeed, a gentlemanly way of leaving a donation for a job well done. The trailer-bridge is not on display on any specific schedule but visitors might be lucky.

The students who built the Dahlenburg covered bridge, worked on the Weddle covered bridge and were involved with the trailer-bridge were in the Building Trades Class of 1989. They were:

Ronald Care	Daniel Conn
Chad Logan	Chris Kennedy
Craig McKay	Brian Nicholson
Kevin Roll	Terry Seiber
David Stegal	Richard Totten

When all the work was finished, the students decided to name the 20-foot bridge over Ames Creek for their teacher, Ben Dahlenburg.

For directions to see these projects, follow directions for Weddle covered bridge.

Name: **Deadwood**   *World Guide* No. 37-20-38
Lane County
Type/Year: Howe   1932
Length: 105 feet   1 span
Spans: Deadwood Creek
Nearest Town: Alpha (site) and Deadwood
Remarks:

Although earlier bypassed by new concrete span about half mile away, the ''severely worn'' covered bridge was rebuilt in 1986 and is again open for traffic, except for trucks over 5-tons. The 1932 bridge had a special deck design with floorboards angled to aid vehicles entering the structure from a curve. The 1990 Status Report by the State says Deadwood covered bridge is in ''excellent shape.''

West of Eugene, highway 126, north from Mapleton to Deadwood. Take Deadwood Creek Road to Deadwood Loop Road, 5.3-miles from post office. Very photogenic bridge.

Name: **Dorena** *World Guide* No. 37-20-23
Lane County
Type/Year: Howe 1949
Length: 105 feet 1 span
Spans: Row River
Nearest Town: Dorena
Remarks:

Town, named for two ladies, Dora Burnett and Rena Martin, is under Dorena Lake but folks moved, with their post office, to present site. This 1948 covered bridge was bypassed in 1974 by a concrete bridge and the covered bridge was abandoned. This bridge's original floor had been paved but the asphalt was pulled up in 1987 as part of a rehab program. Dorena covered bridge remains closed but there are "hopes" that it might be eventually reopened to vehicles. The 1990 State Report observes,"[this bridge] could use some help — no funds requested." Also known as Star Bridge as it once provided access to huge Star Ranch at which there was once a post office.

Exit I-5 at Cottage Grove on the road to Dorena about 12 miles to the bridge. Dorena, Mosby and Stewart covered bridges are in the same neighborhood.

Follow highway 101 from the south end of Lincoln City to Drift Creek Road which is presently marked with a road name sign as well as with a covered bridge marker. Follow this road about 2 miles, watching for direction signs, then go right for half-mile. Pass by the covered bridge to the parking lot on the left.

Name: **Drift Creek**   *World Guide* No. 37-21-14
Lincoln County
Type/Year: Howe   1914
Length: 66 feet   1 span
Spans: Drift Creek
Nearest Town: Cutler City section of Lincoln City
Remarks:

Also known as Upper Drift Creek covered bridge. Although the construction dates are clouded on some bridges, this bridge is accepted as Oregon's oldest. The county is preserving it as a memorial to its pioneers. The bridge is presently the closest to the coast being upstream from highway 101 on winding Drift Creek Road. (Years ago a covered bridge known as Lower Drift Creek covered bridge was on highway 101. It was removed when the Coast Highway was widened.) Due to extensive deterioration, Drift Creek covered bridge is strictly for photographers with no accesss permitted or possible due to substantial barriers. $2,500 in lottery funds provided for rehabilitation study.

53

Name: **Eagle Point*** *World Guide* No. 37-15-02
Jackson County
Type/Year: Queenpost 1922 (moved, rebuilt 1987)
Length: 58 feet 1 span
Spans: Little Butte Creek
Nearest Town: Eagle Point
Remarks:

   *Traditionally known as "Antelope Creek Bridge," was relocated in August 1987 to its present location. Is in good condition with most rehabilitation handled during the move, which was a community-wide event. Because windows were cut into the sides and changed the original specifications, the bridge lost its place on the *National Register of Historic Places.* Also known as Jackson County Bridge 202. Closed to vehicles.

   In City of Eagle Point just east of highway 62, norththeast of Medford.

Site preparation at Eagle Point. Jackson County provided surveyors. Nearby businesses loaned heavy equipment and operators. The plan was to get as much volunteer help, with tools, as possible. The plan was very successful — see next page.

Carcass of Antelope Creek covered bridge enroute to Eagle Point required carefully coordinated help from public and private agencies and many volunteers.

Bridge #202
Eagle Point, Oregon

Originally constructed as Antelope Creek covered bridge on that creek near Eagle Point by Wesley and Lyal Hartman, the bridge was removed then rebuilt in 1987 over Little Butte Creek. (Left) New interior. (Above) Pen sketch by Sue Kupillas shows bridge now in downtown Eagle Point.

Name: **Earnest** *World Guide* No. 37-20-35
Lane County
Type/Year: Howe 1938
Length: 75 feet 1 span
Spans: Mohawk River
Nearest Town: Marcola
Remarks:
  Also called Mohawk River Bridge, and earlier, the Adams Avenue Bridge (1903-1938), present structure was featured in movie "Shenandoah" on a deal that allowed the studio to dress it for Civil War era, then to receive new sides and a paint job when the movie was finished. Again painted in 1987, the bridge is open to regular traffic, with some load restrictions, and is being maintained regularly.

  From Springfield, follow Marcola Road about 17 miles through town to Pachelke Road to the bridge.

Name: **Fisher** *World Guide* No. 37-21-11
Lincoln County
Type/Year: Howe 1919 (1927)
Length: 72 feet 1 span
Spans: Five Rivers
Nearest Town: Fisher
Remarks:

Five Rivers is the alleged name for the river made up of confluence of Alder, Buck, Cherry, Cougar and Crab Creeks and is itself a tributary of Alsea River. *Oregon Geographic Names* recognizes only ''Alsea River.'' This is rugged country. The covered bridge was built in 1919 with repairs of a substantial nature in 1927. The village, Fisher, had a post office from 1892 to 1911, then again from 1912 until 1942. The village and bridge get their name from the ''fisher,'' a small fur-bearing mammal, also known as the marten. The Fisher Elementary school nearby causes the bridge to also be called the Fisher School Bridge now bypassed with a new concrete span. The bridge serves only walkers and bicycles. It is in fair condition considering its little use due to its isolation.

The best route to reach this bridge is west from Corvallis on highway 34 past Alsea then 20 more winding miles to Forest Service Road No. 141, also known as Five Rivers-Fisher Road. Go about 1 mile past Buck Creek Road to the bridge. (Road No. 141 eventually comes out at Deadwood covered Bridge.) Maps show a route over another FS road from Yachats, however, the authors never recommend use of FS or BLM roads without first making local inquiry.

Name: **Fourtner** *World Guide* No. 37-27-03
Polk County
Type/Year: Queenpost 1932
Length: 66 feet 1 span
Spans: South Yamhill River
Nearest Town: Grande Ronde
Remarks:

This private bridge was maintained in good repair for many years and eventually received a tin roof after the hand-split shakes deteriorated. The full name for this span is the Alva "Doc" Fourtner covered bridge. Doc and his wife, Lydia, kept a dairy herd and put up the bridge as means of moving their cattle across the river without risking them in the water. All of the work was done with hand tools. The bridge, never intended for vehicular traffic, accommodates walkers.

From Salem or McMinnville proceed westerly to Grande Ronde which is 2 miles west of Valley Junction. Make turn to north to No. 688A Ackerson Road then left for one block keeping to left at the "Y" and enter the yard at a white house. Obtain permission to proceed to the bridge at the house.

Name: **Gallon House** *World Guide* No. 37-24-01
Marion County
Type/Year: Howe 1916
Length: 84 feet 1 span
Spans: Abiqua Creek
Nearest Town: Silverton
Remarks:

Gallon House covered bridge gets its name from its use as a way-point for running home brew from Mt. Angel, a "wet" town, to Silverton, a "dry" town. There is alleged to have been a "dealer" at the north portal of the covered bridge who appeared by appointment — the north end being in the "wet" territory. Liquor was sold only in gallon jugs, hence the name. This covered bridge is strictly wood from top to bottom. It has a shake roof, wood siding, wood deck, wood approach planks, all perched on wood pilings. The bridge sustained substantial damage in the 1964 Christmas flood but the decision was made to fix it up as an historical attraction, as it was the last covered bridge in the county. The repair lasted another 20 years when, in 1985, a damaged chord caused its closure. Again, the structure, now nearly 70 years old, was repaired but with a 10-ton limit. This is the only covered bridge in Oregon with hinged portals, like a transom that can be raised to allow very high trucks to pass. The September 1990 State Report lists Gallon House covered bridge as undergoing "rebuild ... but no funds yet requested ... will be in excellent shape when [the work] is [finished]."

From Silverton, take highway 214 to the north about a half mile to Hobart Road and turn right for another half mile to the bridge.

Name: Gilkey *World Guide* No.37-22-04
Linn County
Type/Year: Howe 1939
Length: 120 feet 1 span
Spans: Thomas Creek
Nearest Town: Scio
Remarks:

There was once a community named Gilkey that was apparently named for brothers William and Allen Gilkey. It may have been a flag stop on the railroad — the train only stopped when there was farm produce to be picked up — as there is no mention of Gilkey in *Oregon Geographic Names* or in *Oregon Post Offices 1847-1982*. Thomas Creek, over which this span is placed, is big enough to be a river along some of its way with great fishing and swimming holes. The water at Gilkey is host to both. For decades the railroad that parallels the road's bridge was also covered. In the spate of railroad modernization that followed World War II, the rail lines dismantled its roofed bridges, including this one. As Gilkey covered bridge is a general-use span, it enjoys regular maintenance. In 1987, in addition to a coat of paint, some roof work and other nail-pounding, the deck was reinforced as well as some of the pilings.

From Interstate-5, take the Jefferson exit and head for Scio until reaching Robinson Road. Then turn to the southeast to Goar Road and proceed southerly to the bridge where there is limited off-road parking near a pump house.

Name: **Goodpasture** *World Guide* No. 37-20-10
Lane County
Type/Year: Howe   1938
Length: 165 feet   1 span
Spans: McKenzie River
Nearest Town: Vida
Remarks:

Named for the Goodpasture family, who were early settlers, this is the longest covered bridge in service today in Oregon. It's also one of the most photogenic with its long line of windows. The bridge was substantially rebuilt in the 1980's and when finished in 1987, the bridge could handle loaded log trucks once again. All this work, which included new riverside retaining wall and turn lane, rang up a $750,000 bill. Plans for a replacement concrete span were dropped.

On highway 126 about 24 miles east of Springfield.

Name: **Grave Creek** *World Guide* No. 37-17-01
Josephine County
Type/Year: Howe 1920
Length: 105 feet 1 span
Spans: Grave Creek
Nearest Town: Sunny Valley
Remarks:

Named for the fact that young Martha Leland Crowley died and was buried there in 1846 — so named in 1848. Legislature changed name of creek to Leland Creek in honor of the girl but the public didn't like that name. To the present day it's still known as Grave Creek. This valley was the site of Indian trouble in the 1850's thus Fort Leland was established nearby. Post offices operated in the immediate area: Leland, Grave Creek, and finally the people tired of that name and officially renamed it Sunny Valley in 1954. This is Josephine County's only present covered bridge which has great photographic possibilities as there are many camera angles. Recent rumors in the county indicate the bridge might be replaced with concrete, but the public soundly responds: *Nope!*. Recently repainted, the bridge is in good condition.

Grave Creek covered bridge was bypassed when Interstate-5 was constructed but is clearly seen from both north and south lanes as one approaches Sunny Valley exit at the bottom of a broad draw — about 15 miles north of Grants Pass. The bridge is on old highway 99 which is fairly heavily used by rural residents of which the number is growing.

Grave Creek covered bridge in promotional picture for Oregon Stage System bus line probably in early 1930's. (Lower) Carving in Grave Creek bridge was painted over to keep moisture out of the wood. Bridge deck today.

Name: **Hannah** *World Guide* No. 37-22-02
Linn County
Type/Year: Howe   1936
Length: 105 feet   1 span
Spans: Thomas Creek
Nearest Town: Jordan
Remarks:

Named for early pioneer, John Joseph Hannah, who settled there in 1853, it spans Thomas Creek which was named for pioneer Frederick Thomas, who arrived in 1846. Because of its crisp architectural face and accessibility, Hannah covered bridge appeared in numerous television commercials. It's one of several covered bridges that become "diving platforms" for youth in steamy Willamette Valley summers. Hannah covered bridge is in excellent condition.

From Scio, follow on highway 226 to Burmester Creek Road.

Name: **Harris** *World Guide* No. 37-02-04
Benton County
Type/Year: Howe 1929-? (1936)
Length: 75 feet 1 span
Spans: Mary's River
Nearest Town: Wren
Remarks:

Named for the family of George H. Harris, who apparently settled there about 1890. When the post office opened in 1893, name changed to Elam to avoid confusion with Harrisburg, but name, Harris, survives especially for the covered bridge. As with a number of Oregon covered bridges, official records indicate a date when the bridge was built but neighbors assertively disagree, thus there is lively debate whether Harris covered bridge dates from 1929 or 1936. This is the second such bridge at this location. Excellent condition due to use of highway and lottery funds. Very photogenic but snapshooters need to watch for cars that do not slow very much on the sweeping turns at each end of the bridge.

To find this covered bridge, stay on highway 20 west from Corvallis and Philomath to Wren. Watch for direction signs to the bridge

Name: **Hayden** *World Guide* No. 37-02-05
Benton County
Type/Year: Howe 1918
Length: 91 feet 1 span
Spans: Alsea River
Nearest Town: Alsea
Remarks:

Hayden covered bridge is one of several that appear "squat" as the sides are not perpendicular, as some claim, to better let the rain run off. In reality, the designer included flying buttresses for supports and merely angled the sides to cover these protrusions. The windows are high on the sides, "ribbon windows" as some refer to them, reportedly to let some light in. Various covered bridges around Oregon have this feature. On some of the bridges, however, their location might indicate these ribbon-windows are to let the heat out during 100+ degree summer weather. An inspector, quoted in the September 1990 State Report, complained that Hayden covered bridge "needs paint and has rusty roof." Work on the bridge is in progress using highway and lottery funds.

Hayden covered bridge is easily located west of Corvallis on highway 20 turning to highway 34 at Philomath where the road becomes somewhat twisted all the way to Alsea. Look for Hayden Road; follow it a short way to the bridge.

Name: **Hoffman** *World Guide* No. 37-22-08
Linn County
Type/Year: Howe 1936
Length: 90 feet 1 span
Spans: Crabtree Creek
Nearest Town: Crabtree
Remarks:

Hoffman covered bridge was named for the builder, Lee Hoffman, who followed plans provided by the state. This is one of several bridges quite close together. Hoffman had a metal roof and is in fair condition. Has unique bumper on upstream — a metal band — to deflect high water and floating brush and rubbish during runoff. In continual use on a main road, this bridge is kept in good shape. Picturesque.

Easy access from Interstate-5 at Albany on highway 20 to village of Crabtree which has had a post office since 1893, then north on Hungry Hill Road about 1 mile.

Name: **Horse Creek** *World Guide* No. 37-10-12
Douglas County (x Lane County)
Type/Year: Howe 1930 (moved, rebuilt 1990-91)
Length: 105 feet 1 span
Spans: Myrtle Creek (x Horse Creek)
Nearest Town: Myrtle Creek
Remarks:

Several covered bridges have been saved from destruction by valiant preservation efforts and have been dismantled, moved to new locations, then rebuilt. Horse Creek covered bridge is one of these. The bridge got its name when a pioneer group, on coming down the mountain, lost its horses here. In 1968 the highway was realigned and the bridge bypassed. Sheriff patrols had to keep an eye on the bridge as people wanted to live in it. Eventually, because the bridge was deteriorating, the county commissioners decided to take it down in 1986 and give it to Cottage Grove to be rebuilt there. For some reason the gift was declined. The people in Myrtle Creek heard about it — asked for it — got it. A community-wide effort is underway at the present time with dozens of people involved with raising money and pounding nails to rebuild the bridge. The city is providing use of heavy equipment and some manpower. By February 1991 the main frame of the bridge has been assembled and awaits siding and the roof. When the work is completed, the bridge will be hoisted from its work place and positioned over Myrtle Creek adjoining Mill Site Park and a new parking lot yet to be constructed. The work appears to be on schedule with planned reopening, only for pedestrians, in July 1991.

From Interstate-5, take Myrtle Creek exit and stay on Main Street through town on the curved road to the park.

Name: **Irish Bend** *World Guide* No. 37-02-09
Benton County
Type/Year: Howe 1954 (moved 1988)
Length: 60 feet 1 span
Spans: Oak Creek
Nearest Town: Corvallis
Remarks:

Irish Bend gets its name from a tight bend in the Willamette River so named because a number of Irish families took up homesteads there about 1860. This covered bridge originally crossed a slough running more-or-less parallel with, but between the Willamette and Long Tom Rivers, on Irish Bend Road. This is near Monroe. In 1988 the bridge was carefully dismantled, (the pieces numbered and photographed) to make way for a modern concrete span. Many of the original parts, except for those deteriorated by age, were reassembled on new donated piers at the Oregon State University campus in Corvallis. It is presently enjoyed as a pedestrian and bike path over Oak Creek. The project was carried out with donations of $30,000 from the Irish Bend Advisory Committee with matching funds from Benton County. Restoration work used some state lottery money.

Ask for directions at the Information Booth at the entrance to the campus because during school sessions, some campus driveways are restricted to walkers only.

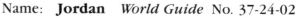

Name: **Jordan** *World Guide* No. 37-24-02
Marion County
Type/Year: Howe   1937
Length: 90 feet   1 span
Spans: Santiam Canal-Salem Power Canal
Nearest Town: Stayton
Remarks:

The bridge was named for the community of Jordan (which had been named for the Jordan Valley in Israel) and spanned Thomas Creek before being relocated to Stayton. The Jordan Bridge Company, a covered bridge preservation group, took charge of fund-raising events and thousands of man-hours before the bridge was ready to serve in its new role as a pedestrian crossing between two parks. One of the fund-raising events was the sale of commemorative bricks on which people's names were impressed. A reserve engineering outfit of the Marines from Salem loaned their skills with the work, then brought in a Marine band on dedication day in 1988.

Find the bridge in Pioneer Park in Stayton.

Name: **Lake Creek** *World Guide* No. 37-20-06
Lane County
Type/Year: Howe 1928
Length: 105 feet 1 span
Spans: Lake Creek
Nearest Town: Greenleaf
Remarks:

    This covered bridge is also known as the Nelson Creek Bridge which refers to a road by that name. Although built in 1928, a major rebuild occurred in 1984 which might make some covered bridge purists cringe. With a now pre-cast concrete deck, it also has a concrete center-pier, trusses repositioned with a crane. Because high-profile loads of logs on trucks had crashed through the low portals, these ''doors'' were enlarged. Today Lake Creek covered bridge looks like new.

    It's east of Deadwood on highway 36 with access from Mapleton on the west, and Junction City to the east.

Name: **Larwood**   *World Guide*   No. 37-22-06
Linn County
Type/Year: Howe   1939
Length: 105 feet   1 span
Spans: At confluence of Roaring River and Crabtree
    Creek
Nearest Town: Lacomb
Remarks:

Larwood covered bridge gets its name from William T.
Larwood who was the local postmaster (1893-1903)
near the bridge. Two uniquenesses are found in its
history: Two earlier covered bridges, only a few feet
apart, crossed both the Roaring River and Crabtree
Creek and, according to *Ripley's Believe It Or Not*, is the
only example of a river emptying into a creek. This
bridge is in good condition and is used primarily by
local traffic.

On Larwood Drive, about four miles to the bridge after
leaving highway 225 from Scio.

The Albany Visitors Association contracted to have
a 14-foot model of Larwood covered bridge built on a
trailer. During summer months, this trailer might be
spotted in various safety rest areas along the freeway being used as an information booth.

VISITORS INFORMATION BOOTH

REPLICA OF THE LARWOOD COVERED BRIDGE BUILT IN 1939, CROSSING CRABTREE CREEK ON FISH HATCHERY ROAD. BUILT USING HOWE TRUSS-TYPE CONSTRUCTION WITH DOUGLAS FIR TIMBER.

This model of Larwood covered bridge mounted on 14-foot long trailer chassis is used as a Tourist Information stand. It is frequently seen in Rest Areas along Interstate-5 during summer. Photographer John Snook, and his wife, Naomi, are standing on left.

75

The Renaissance of a Covered Bridge

Name: **Lost Creek**   *World Guide* No. 37-15-03
Jackson County
Type/Year: Queenpost   1919   (1874)
Length: 39 feet   1 span
Spans: Lost Creek
Nearest Town: Lake Creek
Remarks:

Although challenged many times in its claim to being the shortest covered bridge on an Oregon highway, indeed it is the shortest at only 39-feet. As to its age, while the year 1919 appears on some records, a neighbor and her mother, who have always lived within a stone's throw of the bridge, contend the span was put up between 1874 and 1881. The bridge was nearly lost during the 1964 flood. When first photographed by Bert Webber in 1970, Lost Creek covered bridge was very dilapidated and nearly concealed among spindly trees and weeds. In May 1985, the folks in the Lake Creek community, which includes the bridge, decided to save the bridge as they didn't want it to be trashed without notice as had happened earlier to Yankee Creek covered bridge not far away. They worked together and put on a new roof, braces, and did a general cleaning. Evidence of original construction prior to 1919 is a remark that workers, in 1987, reinstalled new portal boards *"which had been removed in 1919 to allow log trucks to go through without destroying the cover"* — Fred Kildow. In summer 1990, this bridge was hoisted from its old pillars by a loaned crane and set aside so new concrete pillars could be built. When returned to its place, much general renovation was done. Trees were located on private land, felled, then hand-hewn to meet specifications. Much of the work and use of equipment was donated. Of cash needed, $35,000, half came as a result of many fund-raising events spearheaded by Ralph Wehinger, D.C., an avid covered bridge enthusiast. (Dr. Wehinger was instrumental in the planning and installation of Antelope Creek covered bridge over Little Butte Creek in Eagle Point, and worked on the restoration project of McKee bridge, over the Applegate River, earlier.) The other funds came from the Parks and Recreation Department and from state lottery. The bridge is open to pedestrians and bicycles at the present time. There is a concrete span just a few yards away for all vehicles. An agreement was reached whereby the county would make annual inspections and report their findings to the Lake Creek Historical Society which will maintain the bridge.

Out of Medford at the north city limits, take highway 62 then highway 140 to the county road at Lake Creek junction. Follow signs on South Little Butte Creek Road then take Lost Creek Road. This little bridge, on the right, now appears in all its original glory alongside Walch Memorial Wayside Park, in a shaded glen — a private park but open to the public. Photogenic from many angles, particularly in the morning.

Bridge, on blocks, after having been lifted from its old pilings in the creek, awaits new concrete piers. Walch Memorial Wayside, next to site, is quiet, green, cool in mid-summer Rogue River Valley heat.

Lost Creek covered bridge in 1971

Workers lay new deck on the bridge replacing badly worn, plausibly original planks (left inset). After replacing diagonal truss, made from nearby tree, then hand hewn on the site, replacement bolts were installed. Project was partially funded by Oregon State Lottery proceeds along with much local dedication with jobs available for all volunteers (right).

79

Name: **Lowell** *World Guide* No. 37-20-18
Lane County
Type/Year: Howe   1945
Length: 165 feet   1 span
Spans: Middle Fork Willamette River
Nearest Town: Lowell
Remarks:

The original bridge, built in 1907, was not covered. It replaced an earlier ferry. The bridge took the name ''Hyland Ferry Bridge'' for the man who settled there and ran the boat. After a truck wrecked the bridge during World War II, it was rebuilt in 1945 then got its first roof in 1947. In 1953, because of expected high water after the completion of Dexter Dam, both bridge and connecting highway were raised 6-feet. Due to the heavy traffic on the bridge and expectations for ever-increasing loads, the bridge was bypassed in 1981 in favor of a new concrete span. Lowell covered bridge is deteriorating and is closed.

The bridge is off highway 58 near the village of Lowell.

Name:**McKee**   *World Guide* No. 37-15-06
Jackson County
Type/Year: Howe   1917
Length: 122 feet   1 span
Spans: Applegate River
Nearest Town: Ruch   (pron: Roosh)
Remarks:

This span is at 45-feet elevation over a stream classed, as is a river, "navigable," but locals claim the only boats anywhere around are way too big and are pulled on trailers, elsewhere. The river was named for Lindsay Applegate, an early settler who prospected the area. The bridge gets its name from Adelbert (Deb) McKee, who donated the land on which the bridge rests. It is only 8 miles from the California line and from its opening in 1917 until 1956, when it was closed due to deterioration, served regular traffic of miners and loaded logging trucks. The bridge was bypassed by a concrete span. The people wanted to keep "their bridge" so the county, a lodge, and a grange sponsored a new roof. As more years passed and the structure further deteriorated, the county commissioners let it be known that it would take "public support" ($$$) to preserve the bridge. There is an excellent swimming hole at the bridge and a rustic picnic shelter with an immense fireplace made of river rocks. This was built in the 1930's by Civilian Conservation Corps men from nearby Camp Applegate. This shelter continues in use to the present time. The story of the recent McKee Bridge restoration project, which began in 1988, could fill a book. Through hundreds of people's efforts, all sorts of fund-raisers were held and money flowed. McKee Bridge is again in excellent condition and is open for pedestrian enjoyment. The restored bridge is the centerpiece of pride in the McKee Bridge community.

Off highway 238 beyond Ruch, west of Medford and Jacksonville. At Ruch, take Applegate Road following small locally-made signs to the bridge, which presents excellent photo opportunities.

Name: **Milo Academy** *World Guide* No. 37-10-X1
Douglas County
Type/Year: Steel girder   1962
Length: 100 feet   1 span
Spans: South Umpqua River
Nearest Town: Milo
Remarks:

This is a privately owned and maintained covered bridge primarily serving the campus of a Seventh Day Adventist boarding school. There have been three covered bridges at this site, the present structure being unique, as it is a steel bridge with walls and a roof to loosely resemble its forebears. Its simple, rectangular lines have caused some purist covered bridge buffs to shudder. There are narrow, vertical windows cut into the sides for illumination. The bridge stands out from a heavily forested backdrop, thus is a photographer's delight. Milo covered bridge is in good condition.

Leave Interstate-5 at the Canyonville-Days Creek exit. Take highway 227 and drive east about 7 miles to the bridge.

There has been a covered bridge here for just about as long as anyone can remember. Apparently the earliest was for the Bar Lazy Eight Ranch in the 1920's. Date of photo (upper, left) unknown. A different structure is shown in the school's 1958 yearbook (lower). Present bridge (upper and facing page).

Name: **Mosby Creek** *World Guide* No. 37-20-27
Lane County
Type/Year: Howe 1920
Length: 90 feet 1 span
Spans: Mosby Creek
Nearest Town: Cottage Grove
Remarks:

The construction of Mosby Creek covered bridge is unique in that it employs steel rods as cross-braces on upper chords. It is the county's oldest covered bridge but has received continuing maintenance over the years. It was repainted in 1987 and scheduled for overhaul in 1990, but the county delayed the project for at least one year and has not requested funds at the present time. The creek and bridge were named for David Mosby, an early settler who lived near the creek.

After leaving Cottage Grove, continue 1 mile to Mosby Creek Road then to the bridge about 2 miles to the southwest.

Name: **Neal Lane** *World Guide* No. 37-10-07
Douglas County
Type/Year: Kingpost 1929-? (1939)
Length: 42 feet 1 span
Spans: Myrtle Creek
Nearest Town: Myrtle Creek
Remarks:

This is the only kingpost covered bridge in Oregon and has a load limit of 5-tons. As with a number of covered bridges, its construction date is disputed. It crosses Myrtle Creek near that city which was settled in 1851 but not platted as a town until 1865. The name was taken from the so-called ''myrtle'' tree which is really California laurel *(Umbellularia californica)* and common thoughout southwest Oregon and parts of California. Slabs of the wood are beautiful in grain and tool well. Neal Lane covered bridge is in excellent condition.

Off Interstate-5, take Myrtle Creek exit to Main Street, then to Riverside Street for about 1 mile to Neal Lane, go for 1 more mile, to the bridge. Striking photographic opportunities with even the simplest cameras. Excellent condition.

Name: **North Fork Yachats River** *World Guide* No. 37-21-08
Lincoln County
Type/Year: Queenpost 1938
Length: 42 feet 1 span
Spans: North Fork Yachats River
Nearest Town: Yachats (pron. Ya-hotz)
Remarks:

Because the authors class this covered bridge as the most picturesque in Oregon, from a rustic point of view, it graces the cover of this book. The community the bridge serves is isolated and this bridge is the sole access — it's 7 miles from the ocean. But cold, foggy costal weather is missed by the folks here as they are protected by the Coast Range mountains. Although the bridge has seen hard times in the past, (a truck went through a wornout approach in 1987), a general rebuild took place in 1989. The work included new trusses, roof and approaches as well as siding which slopes outward from under the eaves as in many bridges of the area. When the bridge was dedicated in December 1989, the engineer proclaimed his job, if given regular maintenance, should last 50 years.

Access to this very photogenic structure is on the Yachats River Road to the concrete bridge then, on turning to the left for about 2 miles, there is the bridge!

Name: **Office** *World Guide* No. 37-20-39
Lane County
Type/Year: Howe 1944
Length: 180 feet 1 span
Spans: North Fork Willamette River
Nearest Town: Westfir
Remarks:

The Westfir Lumber Company put up this bridge for access between its office, hence the name, and the mill on the other side of the river. Although this bridge was planned as a steel girder bridge, the War Production Board declined a priority for the metal due to the Second World War and directed the company to use wood. This is Oregon's longest covered bridge. To eliminate accidents between pedestrians and vehicles, a separate walking bridge was attached to the outside wall. This walkway was lighted. Office covered bridge is plausibly the heaviest span of its type anywhere, having been designed for heavily loaded logging trucks over a wide stream. It features extra tension rods, huge trusses and extra chords. In the 1980's, a fire leveled the mill and the bridge was closed and the portals equipped with locked gates prohibiting access, even on foot. Although this covered bridge seems worth preserving, the small community appears unable to raise money sufficient to obtain matching funds from the lottery. The future of the deteriorating bridge is in doubt.

From Interstate-5, take highway 58 at Oakridge exit. Turn on Westridge Avenue near milepost 31 and go to Westfir on the county road.

Name: **Parvin** *World Guide* No. 37-20-19
Lane County
Type/Year: Howe 1921 (1986)
Length: 75 feet 1 span
Spans: Lost Creek
Nearest Town: Lowell
Remarks:

From the 1850's homestead of James and Salina Parvin, the original bridge took its name. Replaced in 1921 by the present span, the county closed the bridge to ve-hicles in the 70's when the highway was realigned. It remained open for walkers. Following some cleanup and repair, it was reopened in November 1986 with special ceremonies which granddaughters of the home-steaders attended. Parvin covered bridge handles traffic up to its posted 10-ton limit. The bridge is in excel-lent condition.

From Interstate-5, exit at Goshen and drive about 12 miles on highway 58. Turn right on Lost Creek Road and proceed to the railroad bridge making a right turn onto Parvin Road. The bridge is about 1 mile ahead.

Name: **Pass Creek** *World Guide* No. 37-10-02
Douglas County
Type/Year: Howe 1925 (1989)
Length: 61 feet 1 span
Spans: Pass Creek
Nearest Town: Drain
Remarks:

Pass Creek covered bridge has a colorful history dating from 1870 when it was on the stage route between the Willamette Valley and Jacksonville. The first bridge was apparently replaced about 1906 then again in 1925, the so-called "official" date of the span, when there was a major rebuilding project. The bridge was closed in 1981 due to deterioration then bypassed by a concrete span.

State Report observes the bridge is "owned and recently rebuilt by the City of Drain." It can be viewed in town behind city center at 2nd and West A Streets.

Name: **Pengra** *World Guide* No. 37-20-15
Lane County
Type/Year: Howe 1938
Length: 120 feet 1 span
Spans: Fall Creek
Nearest Town: Jasper
Remarks:

Bridge was named for B.J. Pengra, who was an 1853-arriving pioneer. He became Oregon's general surveyor in 1862. The present structure replaces a bridge that had stood nearby since 1904 and is also known as Fall Creek covered bridge. The lower chords, measuring 16'' x 18'' x 126 feet are the largest single-piece timbers cut in Oregon. They were rough hewn in the forest and finished at the bridge site. The upper chords are 14'' x 18'' x 98 feet. Although bypassed in 1979 due to deterioration, there are restoration plans which will reopen the bridge to traffic. No date for the work has been announced but, as of September 1990, no funds have been requested of the state. Very photogenic

From Springfield, take Oregon highway 22 to Jasper then on Pengra Road go 4 miles to Little Falls Creek Road then turn to the east to Place Road where the bypassed bridge will be seen to the south.

Name: **Remote**   *World Guide* No. 37-06-09
Coos County
Type/Year: Howe 1921
Length: 65 feet 1 span
Spans: Sandy Creek
Nearest Town: Remote
Remarks:

This is one of those covered bridges that had more than one name. While some call it, and file it under "Sandy Creek," there seem to be just as many who call it "Remote" for the village nestled in the trees a few hundred feet away. Remote got its name for being just that — remote from everything else. Its post office opened in 1887 and, with some interruptions, is operating at the present time. This bridge carried all traffic from the coast, including loaded log trucks into Roseburg, thus crossed Howe trusses provided added support. These are easily viewed due to extra large "windows." The bridge was bypassed in 1949 but continued to be an historical attraction. Major cleanup of the bridge and site, a new roof, painting and weed-pulling, now allow an off-highway parking area and picnic opportunities in the old bridge. Bridge is in good condition.

On highway 42, about 30 miles west of Roseburg at the village of Remote. Present highway misses town by a quarter mile, bypasses the bridge by a few feet.

91

Name: **Ritner Creek**   *World Guide* No. 37-27-01
Polk County
Type/Year: Howe   1927
Length: 75 feet   1 span
Spans: Ritner Creek
Nearest Town: Pedee
Remarks:

Determined to be hazardous to users because it was too narrow and traffic much too heavy and faster than the 1927-era Model T Ford it was designed to carry, Ritner Creek's covered bridge was ordered to be replaced. This was the last covered bridge to serve on a primary state highway, thus in March 1976, this era for the highway department closed. The people voted money to save the bridge and to place it in a wayside park only 60 feet away. The little park, with its proud centerpiece, is one of the most photographed covered bridges in Oregon. This is the bridge referred to in the text where nearby residents mounted their rural mail boxes to keep the boxes out of the weather. Although never officially sanctioned, the highway department didn't do anything about it until complaints mounted about people on the bridge being in the way of oncoming traffic. Finally, the post office would no longer serve them so the boxes were removed.

Cross the Willamette River in downtown Salem on highway 22 taking the Dallas exit and drive 17 miles to Dallas. Turn south on highway 223 for 12 miles to the village of Pedee (which once had a post office) then go 3 more miles to the little park.

Name: **Roaring Camp** *World Guide* No. 37-10-11
Douglas County
Type/Year: Howe 1929
Length: 88 feet 1 span
Spans: Elk Creek
Nearest Town: Drain
Remarks:

This covered bridge, which continues to serve limited local traffic, was named for the Roaring Camp Roadhouse nearby. It is also known as the Lancaster Bridge, for the builder. Current evaluation of the bridge in the State Report lists it as "a working, private bridge in sad shape [the few families that depend on it] cannot come up with matching funds for state money — no request for funds."

Out of Drain to the west take highway 38 for 6 miles, find the bridge about 600 feet off the road on left side.

Name: **Rochester** *World Guide* No. 37-10-04
Douglas County
Type/Year: Howe 1933
Length: 80 feet 1 span
Spans: Calapooya River
Nearest Town: Sutherlin
Remarks:

This covered bridge replaces a like bridge here that had been built in the 1860's. The present bridge underwent remodeling in 1969 and is well-maintained, has a 10-ton load limit and is in daily use. Condition: Good. Of significance in appearance are the cathedral-type windows — 4 on each side.

From Sutherlin, follow highway 38 to the west about 2 miles then go north on county road 10-A for 1 mile and see the bridge on a graceful curve in the road.

Name: **Rock O' The Range** *World Guide* No. 37-09-X1
Deschutes County
Type/Year: Timber deck girder 1963
Length: 42 feet 1 span
Spans: Swalley irrigation canal
Nearest Town: Bend
Remarks:

Called Bowerly Road covered bridge by many who use it, this is the only remaining covered bridge in eastern Oregon that is available for both vehicles and pedestrians. It's there because a rancher/land developer liked these structures and decided to have a contractor build one. The bridge crosses the Deschutes Reclamation and Irrigation Canal, called the Swalley Canal as it was named for early settlers Ed and Elmira Swalley. They owned the 1899 water right that allowed the diversion from the Deschutes River into the ditch which runs intermittently in winter and daily in the desert summer. The bridge was built from photograpahs. It is of Douglas fir studs and 6-inch tongue-and-groove vertical siding with a hand-split cedar shake roof. This covered bridge, 42-feet long and 14-feet wide, rests on concrete piers. Load limit: 25-tons. A glance at this bridge might lead some to think this is a kingpost truss, but this non-truss bridge has only angled braces between the studs. The deck is of planks and has added treads over which vehicles cross the span on its single lane. The roof rests on rafters. There is a rectangular window on each wall and long upper ventilator windows under the eaves to let out eastern Oregon summer heat. Bowerly Road is a public road serving the population living along it. The county declines to maintain the bridge, saying it is too small and a liability. The covered bridge's deck is well below the grade of highway 97 and just a few car-lengths from it. The dip causes cars to cross at about 5 miles per hour. Although built with a 12-foot clearance, increased elevation of the highway caused the dip at the east end of the bridge. The safety-clearance is limited to 9 feet, 1 inch, but unobserving truckers crash the portals regularly. Repairs are made by the residents and just about everyone has taken a turn.

Bowerly Road covered bridge is north of Bend's Mountain View Mall on highway 97 about 3 miles north of the city. Watch for large Bowerly Road marker.

Rock O' The Range covered bridge is a fascinating structure. (Left) View of interior north wall shows studs and horizontal and angle braces as well as flooring. (Right) Viewed from southeast corner in winter when vegetation was minimal. Note recently replaced boards in end panel nearest highway, compared with undamaged panel shown on page 95 — opposite end. Photos made Feb. 16, 1991.

Name: **Shimanek** *World Guide* No. 37-22-03
Linn County
Type/Year: Howe 1966
Length: 130 feet 1 span
Spans: Thomas Creek
Nearest Town: Scio
Remarks:

The present bridge is one of the newest in Oregon but is the fifth span at this place on Richardson Gap County Road. The first bridge, 1861, was not roofed but later structures were covered. These were built in 1904, 1921, and 1927. Each could tell a tale of woe. The 1921 bridge came about because its predecessor washed away. Six years later another high water season caused trauma to the piers making the span unsafe. During the Columbus Day storm in 1962, the bridge was badly damaged by falling trees and passage was reduced to 1-lane traffic and load limit only 2-tons. The present bridge has stood since 1966 but has met with a more modern-type of distress. High school boys, with their hot-rods, loved to race down the hill, hit the short, high-angled approach at high speed. A car became airborne, the object being to see how far it would "fly" before thudding onto the deck. There were wrecks and finally a fatal smash. In 1990, the county built new approaches eliminating this risk which never was a hazard to drivers who observed the speed limit. Attractively camera-worthy from many angles.

From Scio, go east 2 miles to Richardson Gap Road, make a left turn and proceed to the bridge.

Name: Short *World Guide* No. 37-22-09
Linn County
Type/Year: Howe 1945
Length: 105 feet 1 span
Spans: South Fork Santiam River
Nearest Town: Cascadia
Remarks:

Gordon Short, who had lived in the area for many years, is remembered with his name on this bridge. The bridge had earlier been known as Whiskey Butte Bridge for a promontory near it. This covered bridge is on scenic highway 20 which, if one had the time and followed it over the mountains, would provide direct access to Rock O' The Range covered bridge on the outskirts of Bend in Deschutes County. Short covered bridge is one of the few in the county with a shake (wood shingle) roof. Recent restoration has included work on the beams and deck, roof, railings and a new paint job. The open ''windows'' help drivers see where they are going and there is a factor, apparently not considered in the early days of covered bridge construction, of resistance of the solid walls to the wind. From a stress standpoint, bridges with open trusses, ''windows,'' should last considerly longer than bridges with solid walls. It might be noted that the Mitchell Bridge in Wheeler County (1917-1952), because of its location in a wind-swept area, had open sides.

Short covered bridge is a distance from Interstate-5, 37 miles to Cascadia (which has a post office continually operating since 1899), then turn on to High Deck Road to the bridge. Quite photogenic.

Name: **Stewart** *World Guide* No. 37-20-28
Lane County
Type/Year: Howe 1930
Length: 60 feet 1 span
Spans: Mosby Creek
Nearest Town: Cottage Grove
Remarks:

Although Lane County announced it had no plan to replace this covered bridge, the inevitable happened when, after decades of damaging incidents, plus the effects of Oregon weather, the bridge was bypassed with a concrete span in mid-1980's. The bridge was almost lost in the winter of 1964 by flood runoff of the creek, then had its roof collapse under heavy snow in 1968. Although out-of-service and blocked, walkers can enjoy the bridge from one end as the approach on the other end was removed for safety. It was repainted in 1987 as part of the county's preservation program. This covered bridge is listed as "in bad shape" and must have major renovation if it is to last.

On leaving Cottage Grove, go 1 mile to Mosby Creek Road. Cross the railroad track then make a left turn. Find bridge at intersection of Garoutte Road and Mosby Creek Road.

Name: **Unity**   *World Guide* No. 37-20-17
Lane County
Type/Year: Howe   1936
Length: 90 feet   1 span
Spans: Fall Creek
Nearest Town: Lowell
Remarks:

Two covered bridges served here, and quite close together, for many years. The original was 129-feet long (Howe) but was closed to vehicles in 1935. It continued in use for walkers until it had deteriorated to a point where it was dismantled in 1953. In the meantime, the new bridge was put up about three quarters of a mile upstream and took the traffic from the older bridge when it opened in 1936.

This bridge is unique as it has a long window on its east side so drivers can watch for oncoming traffic. This window has its own "roof" in an effort to shield motorists eyes from the sun and to keep some of the rain out. This delightful covered bridge is in excellent condition and handles daily traffic. Watch out for photographers!

Highway 58 from Interstate-5 to Lowell, then the Lowell-Unity county road about 2 miles to the bridge.

Name: **Warner Canyon** *World Guide* No. 37-19-X1
Lake County
Type/Year: RR flatcar   1985
Length: 50 feet   1 span
Spans: dry gulch
Nearest Town: Lakeview
Remarks:

This covered span is presently Lake County's only claim to having a covered bridge. Bob Pepperling owned the land and wanted to subdivide and sell a parcel on the other side of a dry gulch so he built this bridge as access to that parcel. For $2,500 he bought the flat car from Southern Pacific Company in Klamath Falls then he paid another $1,000 to have it delivered to his site. This bridge is 9-feet wide and has an overhead clearance of 10-feet. He finished the deck with 4'' x 12'' boards and used 3'' x 12'' stringers. His roof is covered with hand-split shakes. The sides of the covered bridge are rough-sawn cedar boards and batting. At last report (1990), the owner has taken up cattle ranching in Canada and the property was for sale.

From Lakeview, go north on highway 395 to junction with highway 140. Turn into 140 and proceed about 1 1/2 miles. The covered bridge can be seen from the highway. The approaches to the bridge were never finished.

Name: **Weddle**   *World Guide* No. 37-22-05
Linn County
Type/Year: Howe   1937   (1990)
Length: 120 feet   1 span
Spans: Ames Creek (moved from Thomas Creek)
Nearest Town: Sweethome
Remarks:

The county commissioners assigned the name to the bridge but the span has traditionally been known as the Devaney covered bridge for an early resident. It was bypassed by a nearby concrete span in 1980 for vehicles, and the covered bridge was limited to pedestrians and bicycles. In 1987 the bridge was ordered destructed and workers took the order literally. Most of it was hauled away to create a gigantic bonfire. But the trusses remained. A number of interested groups wanted to rebuild the bridge. These included the Covered Bridge Society of Oregon, Cascade Forest Resource Center (organized to rebuild the bridge) and vital assistance from the Jordan Bridge Company, the committee from Stayton that had rebuilt a bridge there. Substantial physical labor on the reconstruction was taken on by the Building Trades class from Sweethome High School, headed by the class's teacher, Ben Dahlenburg. Some lottery money was contributed to the project which was completed in 1989.

On entering Sweethome, on highway 20, make a right turn onto 12th Street at the light and drive 2 blocks then go left in front of the City Hall to Kalmia Street. Go 2 more blocks and note a curve in the road to the right but keep going to Sankey Park where the bridge will be found.

IN TRIBUTE

THE RECONSTRUCTION AND DEDICATION OF THIS BRIDGE IS MADE AS A LASTING TRIBUTE TO SWEET HOME, ITS DEDICATED VOLUNTEERS AND THE PRESERVATION OF OREGON HISTORY.

THE FOLLOWING INDIVIDUALS, BUSINESSES AND ORGANIZATIONS WERE MAJOR CONTRIBUTORS TOWARDS THE SUCCESSFUL COMPLETION OF THIS PROJECT.

BUSINESS AND PROFESSIONAL WOMEN
BETTIE L. CHENNELE
CITY OF SWEET HOME
CLEAR LUMBER COMPANY
COAST CRANE SERVICE, INC.
DAN DARWOOD
FIRST INTERSTATE BANK, INC.
THERON HALEY - HALEY CONSTRUCTION COMPANY
KFIR - KSKD FM
LESTER SALES, INC.
LINN COUNTY
MELCHER LOGGING COMPANY, INC.
MORSE BROTHERS, INC.

GEORGE NEMETI
THE NEW ERA NEWSPAPER - THE PAUL FAMILY
OREGON STATE COVERED BRIDGE RESTORATION FUND
PITTSBURGH PAINT
RICE LOGGING, INC.
PHILL STAFFORD
WES AND SANDY STALEY
S.H.G.P.B.Y.A.R.A.
SWEET HOME HIGH SCHOOL BUILDING TRADES CLASS
SWEET HOME SCHOOL DISTRICT NO. 55
JIM TACK
TRIPLE D EXCAVATING
WILLAMETTE INDUSTRIES, INC.

SPECIAL THANKS TO BEN DAHLENBURG, DON MENEAR AND SCOTT PROCTOR FOR THEIR UNSELFISH COMMITMENT TO THE COMPLETION OF THIS RESTORATION PROJECT

DEDICATED THIS 14th DAY OF JULY, 1990

Weddle covered bridge before and after. (Top) When in service on highway. (Lower) Now for pedestrians in park.

Name: **Wendling**   *World Guide*   No. 37-20-36
Lane County
Type/Year: Howe   1938
Length: 60 feet   1 span
Spans: Mill Creek
Nearest Town: Marcola
Remarks:

This covered bridge got its name from George X. Wendling, director of the Booth-Kelly Lumber Company who established a post office nearby which operated from 1899 until 1952. This older bridge gives off sounds of an earlier time because every time a vehicle rolls along, the planks rumble a greeting. Although the bridge is on a continuous maintanance program and open to traffic, it is classed as "bad shape" and has temporary repairs under its middle. As of September 1990, no repair funds had been requested of the state.

From Interstate-5, exit at Springfield, then take 14th Street (Marcola Road) into Marcola. Take Wendling Road to the east and proceed to the bridge.

Name: **Widing** *World Guide* No. 37-26-X1
Multnomah County
Type/Year: Frame stinger 1965
Length: 38 feet 10 inches 1 span
Spans: East end, Columbia Lake
Nearest Town: Portland
Remarks:

As the bridge appeared in the 1970's.

Sometimes referred to as Oregon's lost covered bridge because many folk, including local residents, don't know it's there, this bridge, also known as Hidden Widing Bridge (private), provides great interest to those who find it. The late Glenn Arn Widing liked covered bridges and he decided to build one that he could see from a window of his mansion. The bridge, on his former private driveway, crossed the east end of Columbia Lake, that end of the lake currently mostly dried up. The bridge frame and sides are in deplorable condition. Although the deck of 2'' x 10'' cross-planks on which there are running strips 6'' x 8'' x 38 feet long, are apparently in good shape due to history of limited usage. Access is so restricted that even the most enthusiastic bridgers are thwarted. There is no accommodation for vehicles. Underbrush has crept over the narrow asphalt driveway to say nothing of the heavy garlands of wild blackberry vines that are hazardous to vehicle paint and are so close together that walking is impeded. The ground, which includes the location of the bridge, is owned by the Port of Portland. In winter, when there are no leaves on the trees, the bridge can be seen from

Marine Drive if one is proceeding eastward and looks to the right just east of the 121st Street N.E. marker — but such glances can be hazardous due to frequent heavy traffic on the road. While the old driveway is just west of the street marker, most vehicles probably cannot negotiate the steep shoulder to get to it and there is no turnaround space at the bottom of the gulch except for a car about the size of a Chevy Geo.

The closest approach to Marine Drive is 122nd Blvd, N.E., north of Sandy Blvd., then west to the abandoned driveway.

Name: **Wildcat Creek** *World Guide* No. 37-20-04
Lane County
Type/Year: Howe 1925
Length: 75 feet 1 span
Spans: Wildcat Creek
Nearest Town: Walton
Remarks:

The picturesque Wildcat Creek covered bridge has seen a lot of traffic in its time and for years was restricted to autos only ("No Trucks") due to 2-ton load restrictions. It has served general traffic in the past and will again when the limit is increased to 20-tons after present renovation is completed. For now, the main use is for local fishermen. The restoration will include new support beams, stringers and new deck. Wildcat covered bridge is west of Eugene on highway 126 near Whitaker Creek-Clay Creek Recreation Area.

Take that exit and pass under the highway and railroad overpass to the bridge

Name: **Wimer** *World Guide* No. 37-15-05
Jackson County
Type/Year: Queenpost 1927
Length: 85 feet 1 span
Spans: Evans Creek
Nearest Town: Wimer
Remarks:

Wimer covered bridge is another with confused dates as to its origin. Some records show a bridge was installed here in 1892 and was replaced in 1927 due to old age and shaky condition. Declared "endangered" again in the early 1960's, the local folks were loud that it be fixed, which it was. A decade later, the bridge again in "trouble," it was closed until a general restoration was undertaken in 1985. The load limit is 8-tons. In 1986, the centennial of the village, where there was a post office between 1887 and 1909, was celebrated with enthusiasm. Some of the landscaping was done by youths under court order for their various misdemeanors. The unique "WIMER" signs on the bridge's portals, white letters on maroon, are said to be from a gas station and are the only signs of this type anywhere on an Oregon covered bridge.

Take Evans Creek Road from city of Rogue River to Wimer — 7 miles.

Beautiful gorge in the mountains that needed a bridge to hook the ends of the road together, is this scene in Upper Rogue River. The most likely place to obtain lumber for these bridges was among the heavy stands of timber at the site. Thus it was done. Picture is taken from a concrete bridge that replaced a covered bridge about one mile south of Prospect in Jackson County. The trees cut for bridge building replaced themselves as this was long before studies of sustained yield and tree farms.

Dickey Prairie Bridge Open For Traffic

DICKEY PRAIRIE (Special) — The Dickey Prairie bridge over the Molalla river, closed recently for repairs, reopened to light traffic late Friday.

The county court signed an order opening the bridge to traffic not exceeding 14,000 pounds and rescinded the previous order closing the span to all traffic.

Load limit signs were posted on both sides of the river.

Meanwhile the court instructed County Surveyor Ralph Milln to survey the area in preparation for major construction work on the bridge.

UPPER LUCKIAMUTE ABOVE HOSKINS, OREGON.

Fate covered bridge (left and lower). Jasper (upper, right) shows new span (white) open for traffic and old span being dismantled.

Two long-gone covered bridges that once spanned Elk Creek. (Top) In town of Elkton. Bridge built 1909 followed earlier covered spans of 1854 and 1979 at same site. Wood for the 1909 bridge had been floated down-river from Kellogg. Bridge lasted until replaced by present concrete span in 1931. (Lower) Hancock Mountain road bridge in use until road bypassed by new tunnel in 1930's. Concrete piers still visible in creek east of tunnel on highway 38.

Cazadero power house and covered bridge over Clackamas River was destination for Saturday and Sunday excursions on electric interurban trains. End-of-track shown in right corner. Picnickers gather to eat in the covered bridge.

Dallas Pumping Station bridge over Rickreall Creek had corregated iron top and sides. It eventually fell into the water and was washed downstream during a storm, undoubtedly the result of lack of maintenance.

(Lower) Old covered bridge that once spanned the North Fork of Coquille River.

(Clockwise) Beaver Creek bridge near Crabtree. Siletz River bridge near Oretown head-end and passing views. Mill Creek bridge in Benton County.

Schooner Creek covered bridge on highway 101 at Taft (top) was replaced by concrete bridge when this main highway was widened after World War II. (Lower) Carver bridge over Clackamas River.

When this bridge was built in 1918 it had to be made of wood due to steel shortage caused by First World War. Classic picture (top) with reflection in John Day River, east of Astoria. (Lower) Deck was hoisted by counterweight in tower.

Note: There are two John Day Rivers in Oregon.

Wagon Bridge on the Santiam at Lebanon, Oregon.

Wagon Bridge on Santiam River at Lebanon was actually three bridges hooked together — the main span over the water plus two short spans, one at each end covering the bridge approaches.

118

"The Covered Bridge" as it was commonly called, was at Mitchell, Wheeler County, over
Bridge Creek. The story goes that the large
windows were to allow the sharp winds to blow
through the span without blowing it over.
(Right) Prairie City covered bridge over John
Day River in Grant County.

Rock Point covered bridge over the Rogue River in Jackson County during construction and finished. This precariously perched structure was eventually replaced with concrete.

120

Mill Creek (there are numerous creeks named "Mill") bridge on Reedsport-Drain highway 38 along Umpqua River. (Lower) Mohawk railroad bridge over Mohawk Creek near Springfield. Saginaw bridge over Coast Fork Willamette River.

Eagle Creek (town) covered bridge over Clackamas River in 1903. This bridge, at 105 feet, was the tallest in Oregon. (Right) Construction of the bridge.

Old covered bridge on Tillamook-McMinnville Stage Road shows four spans, one covered. (Right) Mapleton bridges, new and old. The concrete span was not yet open when the authors visited there in 1974.

South Dillard bridge under construction and finished is one of few 2-span covered bridges. Each span, 144 feet built in 1918. State engineers termed this bridge "Majestic" in appearance. (Right) The Soapstone Creek bridge in Clatsop County.

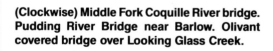

(Clockwise) Middle Fork Coquille River bridge. Pudding River Bridge near Barlow. Olivant covered bridge over Looking Glass Creek.

Siletz-Logsdon covered bridge in earliest picture (lower, left) built in 1922 — 100-foot span — over Sams Creek. It was bypassed by concrete but the old bridge was left in place (right) as a monument to the past.

The "late" Yankee Creek covered bridge was hauled down without public notice on Apr. 3, 1974 by Jackson County workers to make way for a concrete span. The top and sides were consumed by roadside bonfire within hours. The bridge was one of many built by Wesley and Lyal Hartman. (Top) As it stood the morning of Apr. 3. (Lower left) As it stood at dusk Apr. 3. (Lower right) The authors salvaged these mementoes from remnants of the fire on Apr. 5.

There appears to be confusion whether these scenes are in Clackamas County on Sandy River or in Multnomah County on Bull Run River, as much of the property has been "off limits" to the public for decades because it is in the watershed of the City of Portland. Authors lean toward Clackamas County. Is this village that of Bull Run? In picture below, note gasoline pump in front of store which had a public telephone. The Bullrun (1 word) post office operated between 1895 and 1939 plausibly in this building. Photos taken Aug. 14, 1924.

Elk City covered bridge was the centerpiece of a serene village on Yaquina River. While work was underway to renovate the bridge, with part of the funds provided by the Covered Bridge Society of Oregon, a windstorm came up and the bridge fell into the water from temporary abutment. The structure was totally wrecked during effort to raise the bridge.

(Top to bottom, left to right) Private bridge over East Creek, Tillamook County. Stephens Bridge, Calapooya Creek — 1903. Little River bridge at Glide. Murder Creek bridge. Thomas Creek bridge near Jordan.

(Top) Winona covered bridge in Josephine County along Jump-off Joe Creek. (Left) Inked lines show where State Highway Department planned to build concrete span which eventually came to pass. Site is on Butte Falls-Prospect road. Is believed to be over Beaver Creek in Jackson County.

This covered bridge over the Upper Rogue River, about one mile south of Prospect, is probably the last of several covered spans at this site. A concrete span now served this crossing. According to the postcard's message:

Roseburg Feb. 14, '09
In the spring of 1906, I kicked the middle plank off this bridge so people could see down the river. Yesterday when I bought some cards, I told the clerk and he said a man told the same story a few days ago. Who lied? This is near Prospect.

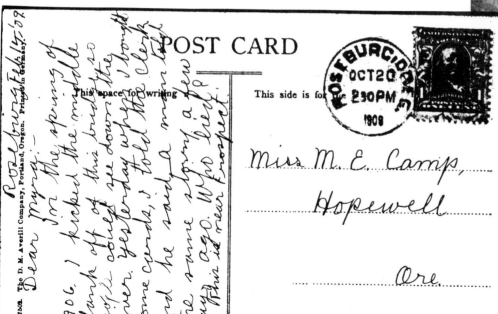

POST CARD

ROSEBURG ORE OCT 20 2:30PM 1908

This side is for the writing

Miss M. E. Camp,

Hopewell

Ore

This space for writing

752A. The D. M. Averill Company, Portland, Oregon. Printed in Germany.

Roseburg Feb. 14, '09
Dear Myra:
In the spring of 1906, I kicked the middle plank off of this bridge so people could see down the river. Yesterday when I bought some cards, I told the clerk and he said a man told the same story a few days ago. Who lied? This is near Prospect.

157161

Which Bridge is Which?
The *World Guide* Number System

Because bridge types, names of streams bridges cross, local names given to bridges, and other identifying factors are often the same, it became necessary for a scheme of identification to be established where each bridge would be clearly different from any other in the manner it is identified. Accordingly, the World Guide Covered Bridge Numbering System was developed. Credit for this system of international importance, is given to Philip and Betsy Clough. The system was adopted by the National Society for the Preservation of Covered Bridges.

In making up the numbers for each bridge, three elements are considered for covered bridges in the United States. The format 00-00-00 is followed.

The first block of two numbers identifies the state in alphabetical order with 01 assigned to Alabama; 05 assigned to California; 37, which this book is concerned with — Oregon.

The second block is for county identification. In Oregon, 01 is for Baker County but as there are no present covered bridges in that county, 01 does not appear in this book. Benton County therefore is 02 and is found herein.

The third block of two-digit numbers locates the bridge within a county. This section of the overall number considers that some bridges will be taken down or destroyed thus, the number goes with the bridge — is not reused.

In this book there are several bridges that do not have World Guide Numbers because they have not been considered a "true truss-supported" bridge. For the purposes of this book, the local bridge number — the third set of digits — is represented by the letter **X** if it was omitted from the World Guide numbering system. Following the X are numbers starting with 1, as X1, for the first such bridge identified in a county. If there is a second or third bridge in this classification, then subsequent numbers appear as X1, X2, X3, etc.

Appendix
Index of Covered Bridges in Oregon - 1947
Oregon State Highway Department
286 Bridges in this List

This inventory is Noted for its Omissions

Road No.	Milepost	Date Built	Name	Stream

Note: To save space: Fork, Creek, River, North, South are shown as Fk Ck Riv No So

Benton County (18)

Road No.	Milepost	Date Built	Name	Stream
27	39.16	None	Flynn	Mill Crk
27	59.0	1922	Noon's	Marys Riv
33	50.15	None	-	Marys Riv
190	17.15	None	-	Luckiamute Riv
190	24.90	1922	-	Marys Riv
201	00.1	-	-	Alsea Riv
0-2	00.2	1935	-	Marys Riv
0-2	2.5	1929	-	Marys Riv
0-4	0.8	Unknown	-	Marys Riv
532	0.1	Unknown	-	Lemon Ck
624	0.7	1906	-	Marys Riv
752	0.25	Unknown	-	No Fk Alsea Riv
773	1.7	Unknown	-	Long Tom Riv
773	5.85	Unknown	-	Long Tom Riv
818	5.1	Unknown	-	Long Tom Riv
501	1.9	1923	-	Big Luckiamute Riv
502	1.8	1930	-	Big Luckiamute Riv
502	0.7	-	-	Big Luckiamute Riv

Clackamas County (15)

Road No.	Milepost	Date Built	Name	Stream
M-9	11.3	Unknown	-	Butte Ck
570	0.8	-	-	Molalla Riv
571	2.0	Unknown	-	Pudding Riv
626	0.9	Unknown	-	Rock Ck
632	1.29	Unknown	-	Butte Ck
665	4.5	Unknown	-	Rock Ck
692	0.3	Unknown	-	Butte Ck
890	1.8	1920	-	Molalla Riv
903	4.7	Unknown	-	No Fk Molalla Riv
908	0.0	1913	-	Molalla Riv
923	0.0	Unknown	-	Butte Ck
1038	0.8	Unknown	-	Milk Ck
1154	1.9	Unknown	-	Sandy Riv
1253	0.4	Unknown	-	Sandy Riv
1310	1.0	Unknown	-	Sandy Riv

Clatsop County (1)

Road No.	Milepost	Date Built	Name	Stream
9	40.94	-	-	No Fk Nehalem Riv

Coos County (3)

Road No.	Milepost	Date Built	Name	Stream
35	19.90	1922	-	Big Ck
35	27.21	1921	-	Sancy Ck
35	29.36	1219	-	Rock Ck

Douglas County (39)

Road No.	Milepost	Date Built	Name	Stream
35	41.97	1922	-	Coquille Riv
35	52.37	1922	-	Lower Ten Mile Ck
35	56.01	1922	-	Looking Glass Ck
35	60.93	1922	-	Looking Glass Ck

Road No.	Milepost	Date Built	Name	Stream
45	13.19	1925	-	Mill Ck
230	20.6	-	-	Coffey Ck
231	24.15	-	-	Calapooya Ck
0-3	7.0	1928	-	Mill Ck
0-3	13.05	1932	-	Lake Ck
M-4	19.55	1924	Lone Rock	No Umpqua Riv
M-4	24.35	1921	-	Rock Ck
0-9	2.0	1905	-	Calapooya Ck
0-9	10.85	1910	-	Hubbard Ck
504	8.4	1904	-	Calapooya Ck
504	13.6	1904	-	(not identified)
504	14.2	1904	-	Hinckle Ck
504	14.6	1904	-	Calapooya Ck
506	2.8	1930	-	Calapooya Ck
528	0.0	-	-	So Umpqua Riv
546	0.8	1905	-	Calapooya Ck
546	11.3	1910	-	Calapooya Ck
564	9.2	-	-	So Umpqua Riv
579	0.2	1916	-	Elk Ck
589	1.0	-	-	Calapooya Ck
589	1.1	None	-	(not identified)
607	1.1	1900	-	Deer Ck
620	2.1	1924	-	Cow Ck
633	0.2	1923	-	Cow Ck
641	0.2	1913	-	Cow Ck
671	0.8	1916	-	So Umpqua Riv
671	4.9	1905	-	Looking Glass Ck
671	8.09	-	-	Looking Glass Ck
673	3.2	1907	-	Looking Glass Ck
674	0.4	1919	-	Looking Glass Ck
680	0.0	1922	-	Roberts Ck
684	0.2	1924	-	So Umpqua Riv
697	4.4	1915	-	Cow Ck
734	2.05	1936	-	Olalla Ck
751	16.4	1931	-	No Fk Smith Riv

Grant County   (1)

Road No.	Milepost	Date Built	Name	Stream
5	171.40	1917	Prairie City	John Day Riv

Hood River County   (1)

Road No.	Milepost	Date Built	Name	Stream
534	0.8	-	-	East Fk Hood Riv

Jackson County   (5)

Road No.	Milepost	Date Built	Name	Stream
527	0.6	-	-	Antelope Ck
859	9.69	-	-	Beaver Ck
865	6.19	-	-	Applegate Riv
927	1.81	1921	-	Thompson Ck
980	1.2	-	-	Rogue Riv

Lane County   (92)

Road No.	Milepost	Date Built	Name	Stream
18	10.02	1923	-	Lost Ck
34	53.50	1921	-	Long Tom Riv
34	54.05	1921	-	Long Tom Riv
201	14.5	-	-	Deadwood Ck
220	.05	1919	-	Siuslaw Riv
220	32.4	-	-	(unidentified)
501	9.25	-	-	Mohawk Riv
501	15.4	1917	-	Mohawk Riv
501	18.95	-	-	Mill Ck
504	4.9	1925	-	Camp Ck
512	1.1	1923	-	(unidentified)
521	9.15	1916	-	Overflow Channel McKenzie Riv
531	0.4	1917	-	McKenzie Riv
533	0.1	1916	-	Mohawk Riv
553	0.3	1917	-	Mill Ck
553	1.5	1903	-	Mohawk Riv
562	2.3	-	-	(unidentified)
569	1.38	1926	-	Salmon Ck
570	1.9	1932	-	Hills Ck
571	6.1	1929	-	Little Falls Ck
571	8.2	1890	-	Big Falls Ck
571	11.6	1907	-	Willamette Riv
583	0.1	-	-	Fall Ck
585	1.6	1932	-	Winberry Ck
587	22.55	-	-	No Fk Willamette Riv

Road No.	Milepost	Date Built	Name	Stream
588	2.7	1923	-	Lost Ck
588	5.3	--	-	No Fk Lost Ck
591	4.45	1921	-	Lost Ck
597	8.8	-	-	Teeter Ck
597	19.0	1904	-	Row Riv
597	21.8	1935	-	Frank Brice Ck
597	22.9	1930	-	Frank Brice Ck
597	28.1	-	-	Champion Ck
600	9.0	-	-	Sharps Ck
600	11.3	-	-	Sharps Ck
600	18.15	1928	-	Row Riv
610	0.0	1930	-	Mosby Ck
610	3.25	-	-	Row Riv
614	0.1	-	-	Mosby Ck
621	20.45	1917	-	McKenzie Riv
632	0.5	-	-	Mohawk Riv
636	2.85	1928	-	Row Riv
660	0.0	-	-	East Fk Five Riv
660	0.4	-	-	West Fk Five Riv
661	0.2	1934	-	(unidentified)
681	2.2	-	-	Mill Race
715	0.15	-	-	Coast Fk Willamette Riv
723	0.15	1920	-	Mosby Ck
723	1.35	1025	-	Row Riv
764	1.95	1930	-	Coast Fk Willamette Riv
764	5.75	1917	-	Coast Fk Willamette Riv
764	10.8	1925	-	Coast Fk Willamette Riv
788	0.05	1923	Miller	Coast Fk Willamette Riv
789	1.4	-	-	Coast Fk Willamette Riv
790	0.05	1934	-	Coast Fk Willamette Riv
790	0.4	-	-	Saroute Ck
835	2.7	-	-	Saroute Ck
835	2.4	1916	-	Saroute Ck
835	3.0	1934	-	Saroute Ck
843	0.4	-	-	Saroute Ck
843	0.5	-	-	Saroute Ck
844	0.25	-	-	Saroute Ck

Road No.	Milepost	Date Built	Name	Stream
890	0.8	-	-	Slough
988	3.6	-	-	Bear Ck
1040	9.8	-	-	Noti Ck
1041	6.95	1917	-	Wolf Ck
1041	26.65	1925	-	Siuslaw Riv
1041	27.6	1925	-	Siuslaw Riv
1041	31.1	1926	-	Wolf Ck
1041	39.6	1925	-	Wildcat Ck
1057	0.05	1917	-	Siuslaw Riv
1071	0.75	1930	-	Long Tom Riv
1075	5.8	-	-	(unidentified)
1095	11.2	-	-	Lake Ck
1098	0.1	-	-	Deadwood Ck
1106	0.0	-	-	Deadwood Ck
1106	1.4	-	-	West Fk Deadwood Ck
1111	22.5	192	-	West Fk Deadwood Ck
1112	18.3	-	-	No Fk Siuslaw Riv
1112	20.8	1930	-	No Fk Siuslaw Riv
1115	5.5	1930	-	No Fk Siuslaw Riv
1115	5.6	1924	-	No Fk Siuslaw Riv
1115	8.7	1930	-	Condon Ck
1115	11.9	-	-	No Fk Siuslaw Riv
1115	14.3	1928	-	McLeon Ck
1116	1.9	-	-	Knowles Ck
1117	0.0	1935	-	Siuslaw Ck
1168	0.35	-	-	Salt Ck
1168	2.0	1926	-	Hills Ck
1171	0.0	1905	-	McKenzie Riv
1173	0.1	1907	-	McKenzie Riv
1173	1.25	1931	-	Horse Ck

Lincoln County (37)

Road No.	Milepost	Date Built	Name	Stream
9	120.94	1924	-	Salmon Riv
27	7.22	1925	-	Alsea Riv
180	11.8	-	-	Yaquina Riv
181	20.6	1922	-	Siletz Riv
181	23.1	1922	Fuller	Siletz Riv

Road No.	Milepost	Date Built	Name	Stream
506	1.3	-	-	Slick Rock Ck
508	3.8	-	-	Salmon Riv
515	2.8	-	-	Drift Ck
515	4.4	-	-	Schooner Ck
527	0.6	-	-	Mill Ck
531	5.7	-	-	Siletz Riv
542	7.9	-	-	Siletz Riv
542	12.8	-	-	Big Rick Ck
560	9.5	-	-	Drift Ck
560	10.3	-	-	Drift Ck
564	0.0	-	-	Big Elk Ck
568	2.7	-	-	Yaquina Riv
568	5.0	-	-	Big Elk Ck
568	8.2	-	-	Big Elk Ck
568	19.1	-	-	Deer Ck
569	0.0	-	-	Yaquina Riv
572	22.7	-	-	Big Elk Ck
579	0.0	-	-	Alsea Riv
579	10.4	-	-	Little Lobster Ck
580	2.9	-	-	Cascade Ck
580	3.6	-	-	Five Riv
582	7.2	-	-	Yachats Riv
582	9.2	-	-	Yachats Riv
582	9.5	-	-	Yachats Riv
582	9.7	-	-	Yachats Riv
582	10.1	-	-	Yachats Riv
583	0.0	-	-	Five Riv
583	2.1	-	-	Buch Ck
605	0.1	-	-	Yaquina Riv
612	0.0	-	-	Elk Ck
1105	0.0	-	-	Five Riv
1101	13.0	-	-	Big Lobster Ck

Linn County (53)

Road No.	Milepost	Date Built	Name	Stream
211	15.48	-	-	Thomas Ck
212	11.8	-	-	Calapooya Riv
212	12.8	-	-	Calapooya Riv
M-2	39.2	-	-	Owl Ck
M-3	2.0	-	-	Muddy Ck
0-7	2.3	-	-	(unidentified)
M-13	6.9	1914	-	Calapooya Riv
M-25	4.65	1916	-	Crabtree Ck
M-26	1.1	1913	-	Walton Slough
M-28	2.6	1936	-	Thomas Ck
505	1.7	-	-	So Santiam Riv
513	2.32	1913	-	Crabtree Ck
525	1.15	1935	-	No Santiam Riv
669	5.1	-	-	Little Muddy Ck
688	1.1	-	-	Muddy Ck
735	0.2	-	-	(unidentified)
748	0.55	1911	-	Albany Ditch
759	0.21	1929	-	Albany Ditch
760	0.55	1911	-	Albany Ditch
761	1.95	1931	-	Albany Ditch
761	2.85	1912	-	Oak Ck
769	1.55	1911	-	Oak Ck
777	2.9	1911	-	Albany Ditch
797	0.4	1910	-	Calapooya Riv
811	0.4	1910	-	Sodom Ditch
811	0.85	1910	-	slough [sic]
812	0.55	1913	-	Sodom Ditch
812	1.4	1916	-	Sodom Ditch
895	1.6	1912	-	Muddy Ck
936	3.05	1912	-	Thomas Ck
946	.8	-	-	(unidentified)
966	1.35	1934	-	Crabtree Ck
1007	2.55	1912	-	Albany Ditch
1014	0.9	1915	-	Lebadon Canal*
1014	6.2	1912	-	Albany Ditch
1022	1.04	1912	-	Albany Ditch
1038	0.8	1912	-	Lebadon Ditch*
1165	0.74	1922	-	Thomas Ck
1173	0.0	1910	-	Neal Ck

* May mean Lebanon

Road No.	Milepost	Date Built	Name	Stream
1217	3.35	1915	-	Roaring Riv
1217	3.31	1916	-	Crabtree Ck
1286	2.9	1916	-	So Santiam Riv
1286	5.8	1910	-	McDowall Ck
1300	0.0	-	-	Calapooya Riv
1322	3.5	1925	-	Calapooya Riv
1350	0.02	1915	-	Thomas Ck
1355	0.03	1890	-	Thomas Ck
1371	1.27	1917	-	So Fk Neal Ck
1423	0.05	1936	-	Middle Fk Santiam Riv
1425	0.8	1911	-	So Santiam Riv
1437	0.7	-	-	Wiley Ck
1474	4.9	-	-	No Santiam Riv
1490	10.3	-	-	So Santiam Riv

Marion County (10)

Road No.	Milepost	Date Built	Name	Stream
610	3.8	1907	-	Pudding Riv
616	12.8	-	-	Abiqua Ck
616	13.8	1935	-	Abiqua Ck
628	3.0	-	-	Pudding Riv
657	0.8	-	-	Abiqua Ck
662	1.6	-	-	Silver Ck
664	2.9	-	-	Abiqua Ck
741	7.45	-	-	Abiqua Ck
795	1.1	-	-	Mill Ck
918	2.8	-	-	Mill Ck

Polk County (3)

Road No.	Milepost	Date Built	Name	Stream
190	15.12	-	-	Ritner Ck
191	6.7	-	-	Luckiamute Riv
994	0.4	-	-	Luckiamute Riv

Tillamook County (4)

Road No.	Milepost	Date Built	Name	Stream
0-2	0.7	-	-	Trask Riv
0-3	17.55	-	-	Nestucca Riv
0-18	0.4	-	-	Nestucca Riv
569	0.3	-	-	East Ck

Road No.	Milepost	Date Built	Name	Stream
Wheeler County (1)				
41	68.42	1917	-	Bridge Ck
Yamhill County (3)				
526	0.9	-	-	No Yamhill Riv
578	6.2	-	-	Coast Ck
582	0.0	-	-	Willamina Ck

Oregon Covered Bridges
and the
National Register of Historic Places

According to a study made by the Oregon Department of Transportation in 1986, all covered bridges in Oregon were either eligible for or listed on the *National Register of Historic Places* with three exceptions:

Cavit Creek covered bridge
Bohemian Hall covered bridge
Shimanek covered bridge

Of those on the list, two have been deleted:

Antelope Creek covered bridge, dropped due to change of the design when relocated.
Dallas Pumping Station covered bridge, dropped due to collapse — total wreck.

Senate Interim Committee on Transportation
Concepts for a New Covered Bridge Bill

Submitted by Senator Mae Yih

What started out as a small idea between myself and Don Rhodewalt, to save two Linn County covered bridges, has resulted in not only saving those bridges but in addition has turned into a preservation effort for all 52 covered bridges in Oregon. The State Covered Bridge Program has or will assist in the current complete rebuilding of four bridges (Irish Bend, Weddle, North Fork Yachats, Gallon House) and the repair/maintenance of twenty bridges since its inception in 1989.

Continued requests are coming in to Oregon for information on our covered bridges and the rebuilding effort. Although Oregon ranks 5th in total covered bridges within its borders, Oregon is THE LEADER regarding its restoration efforts on these historic resources. This has garnered nationwide recognition. Last month one bridge, near Scio, (Gilkey) was the scene of a major advertising effort. After two days of videotaping, this bridge will appear on national television in the background of a Ford truck commercial.

The Dept. of Transportation and lottery funds supply the monies currently used for these rebuilding efforts. The continued requirement of relying on these sources for funds places this effort in a tenuous position. No long term plans (over two years) can be made and one never knows how much lottery money will be available. I believe a Senate Bill is the answer to this problem and have outlined, on the following pages, the parameters for such a Bill. My hope is that you will see the necessity for and will, in fact, lead your peers in sponsoring this Bill.

I also enclose for your use a complete status of all the covered bridges within Oregon — their physical shape and lottery and Dept. of Transportation funding used on each bridge.

Current Covered Bridge Status — Sept. 27, 1990

An inventory conducted by Bill Cockrell, a leader in the Covered Bridge Society of Oregon, during a tour of the bridges in summer 1990 with members of the National Society for the Preservation of Covered Bridges. The data for those bridges in Linn County was furnished by Don Rhodewalt of Linn County.

Harris — In good shape, county did work on bridge several years ago. Repair work currently being done using highway and lottery funds.

Hayden — Needs paint and has rusty roof. Repair work currently being done using highway and lottery funds.

Irish Bend — Newly restored using private and county resources. Restoration work used some lottery funds.

Remote — In good shape, rebuilt in 1983. Repair work currently being done using lottery funds.

Rock O' The Range — Pseudo covered bridge. No request for funds.

Cavitt Crk — Chords and approaches need work. No request for funds.

Milo Academy — Pseudo covered bridge. In good shape. Repair work being done using lottery funds.

Neal Lane — Repaired recently by county without state funds (new floor, etc.). No request for funds.

Pass Crk — Owned and recently rebuilt by the city of Drain. No request for funds.

Roaring Camp — Is a working, private bridge in sad shape. Cannot come up with matching funds for state money. No request for funds.

Rochester — Looks good. Has about a 10 ton limit. Has concrete approaches. No request for funds.

Antelope Crk — Rebuilt in 1987 and is in good shape. [Moved to Eagle Point.] Some repair work being done with lottery funds.

Lost Creek — Being worked on right now — replacing some chords. [Portion of] repairs [was] done with lottery funds. [Work completed fall 1990.]

McKee — Rebuilt last spring. Applied directly to the lottery fund on their own. Did not use state program funds. No request for funds.

Wimer — Spent about $40,000 on bridge in 1985. Needs no help. No request for funds.

Grave Crk — Seems to be in good shape, needs cosmetic (paint, boards) work. No request for funds.

Belknap — In daily use and in good shape. No request for funds.

Chambers RR — Privately owned and in sad shape — can't locate owner. No funds requested, however, will need help next year.

Coyote Crk — In good shape, used daily — worked on about 3 years ago. No funds requested.

Currin — Bypassed by the county and needs help. No funds requested.

Deadwood Crk — Rebuilt in 1987 (about $200,000) and in excellent shape. No funds requested.

Dorena — Bypassed by the county and could use some help. No funds requested.

Earnest — Currently being worked on using lottery funds. Requested lottery funds to help with repairs.

Goodpasture — Rebuilt several years ago ($750,000) and in good shape. No funds requested.

Lake Creek — Rebuilt in 1983/84 (new piers and floor) and in excellent shape. No funds requested.

Lowell — Bypassed by the county and needs help. No funds requested.

Mosby Crk — Needs help but Lane County requested waiting till next year. No funds requested.

Office — In bad shape and needs help but community can't raise matching funds. No funds requested.

Parvin — Rebuilt in 1987 and in excellent shape. No funds requested.

Pengra — Bypassed by the county and needs help. No funds requested.

Stewart — Bypassed by the county and now in bad shape. No funds requested.

Unity — In good shape, used daily. New floor several years ago. No funds requested.

Wendling — In bad shape — has temporary repair under the middle. No funds requested.

Wildcat Crk — Being rebuilt this year using lottery money. Lottery funding requested.

Chitwood — Rebuilt several years ago and in good shape. No funds requested.

Fisher School — Roof and siding repaired several years ago. Trusses and piers may need work shortly. No funds requested.

North Fork Yachats — Completely rebuilt prior to applying to state fund. Will probably request the limit on lottery funds.

Drift Crk — Needs help badly. Lottery funding paid for $2500 study. No request yet but need study results to determine the cost.

Crawfordsville — Needle beam replaced and bridge is in good shape now.

Requested use of lottery funds.

Gilkey — Needs some repair which will be done this fall. Requested highway and lottery funds.

Hannah — In excellent shape, recent repairs used both funds. Requested highway and lottery funds.

Hoffman — In fair shape but will use funding for repairs this fall. Requested highway and lottery funds.

Larwood — In good shape but will do some repair using both funds. Requested highway and lottery funds.

Shimanek — Recently repaired and in good shape. Used both funds. [New approaches in fall 1990 completed.] Requested highway and lottery funds.

Short — In fair shape but heavy repair put off till next year. Requested highway funds only. Will need lottery funds next year.

Gallon House — Complete rebuild in progress but no funds yet requested. Bridge will be in excellent shape when [work] is [finished]. No request for funds but will probably go for maximum lottery funds when their bills come in.

Jordan — In excellent shape. Moved and rebuilt in 1987/88. Needs cosmetics. Requested lottery funds.

Cedar Crossing — Pseudo covered bridge. Doesn't need any funds. No request for funds.

Ritner Crk — Moved in 1976, needs some cosmetic (paint, etc.) work. Requested lottery funds.

Horse Crk — Being rebuilt by volunteers with the city of Myrtle Creek. Replacing the upper chords. Requested lottery funds.

Weddle — This bridge started [the major thinking about covered bridge preservation. It was] moved and rebuilt in 1989/90 by volunteers in the city of Sweet Home. Requested and used lottery funds.

Bohemian Hall — Will very shortly be moved from [storage] near Scio to Albany where it will be rebuilt using volunteer help and lottery funds. Requested lottery funds.

Senate Covered Bridge Bill — Outline

1. Continue the usage of Dept. of Transportation funds for the maintenance of those bridges which are publically owned and carry vehicle traffic. This program will require inspections and a 50% matching fund from the bridge owner to qualify. The current funding is $5642 per bridge per biennium.

2. Allot $350,000 from the General Fund over the next biennium for major restoration work on any of the state's 52 covered bridges. This again will require an inspection program and 50% matching funds from the bridge owner to qualify for the funds. All of this alloted money *may not* be used. Completion of this biennium, however, should see all the major covered bridge work completed and this Senate Bill used to insure good maintenance procedures. *Note:* Administrative costs shall not be taken from the funding figures in Nos. 1 and 2.

3. Bypassed bridges: Frequently, as in Lane County, bridges are bypassed by the regular road and this results in the slow decline in the life of the bridge. Very little further effort is made to retain its load carrying capacity. A requirement shall be written into this Bill which requests that every possible effort be made to upgrade the load carrying capacity of the bridge during any major rebuilding effort. Using this criteria, the bypassed bridges could ultimately be brought back to their normal function — carrying vehicles on roadways rather than pedestrians in walkways.

4. Continue the usage of the Covered Bridge State Advisory Committee. Their task, as it is now, will be to review and approve the paperwork associated with the bridge program.

5. Two bridges within the state are real "hardship cases." They are:

Roaring Camp — Drain, Oregon
Office — Westfir, Oregon

These bridges are located in communities with very little financial base and population. They are both privately owned bridges. Repeated efforts to raise the required 50% matching funds have failed. Without some extra effort from the state, these bridges will be lost. As privately built bridges, their configuration is unique and totally unlike other bridges within the state, yet they are true covered bridges. For this reason, the Bill will carry "hardship case" funding allowing the matching funds in these cases to drop to 10% rather than the normal 50%. As mentioned before, without this deviation, these unique bridges will be lost.

Covered Bridge Status Report

Submitted by Chris Ledeham

September 1990

In the 1920's, the State of Oregon had over 400 covered bridges. Today only 52 [*sic*] remain. [*Authors' Note:* Recall that this Senate Report concerns covered bridges on public roads while this book includes all standing covered bridges including some on private property and those built "unconventionally" — on railroad flatcars. The number of bridges reported in this section refer only to those defined in this section.]

In light of their dwindling numbers, the 1987 Legislative Emergency Board appropriated $25,000 to the Parks Department for a study of Oregon's covered bridges. The directive was to assess the condition of the remaining covered bridges and make recommendations on how the legislature can assist in preserving them.

This study identified Oregon as having the largest collection of covered bridges west of the Mississippi River. We are sixth in the nation. It estimated that over $600,00 of repair work was immediately needed for these bridges. $2,250,000 would be required over a 20-year period. Of these 52 bridges identified, 25 were in good condition, 12 were in fair condition, 12 were in poor condition and 3 were in storage.

In response to the study, a program was established under House Bill 3075 which provided funds from lottery revenues. This program is dedicated to the rehabilitation of all covered bridges. A second source of monies was secured by using highway funds. These are dedicated to the maintenance of publically owned covered bridges in vehicular service. Both programs are on a 50-50 matching fund basis and extend through this current biennium.

Highway Funds

$158,000 of highway funds were set aside for maintenance of covered bridges. Maintenance includes activities such as roofing, painting, deck replacement and annual inspections. Reimbursement is strictly limited to the covered portion of the bridge. Since these are transpsortation dollars, only publically owned bridges open to vehicular traffic are eligible. Of our 52 bridges, 28 fit this criteria. Each bridge has been allotted $5,642. Since painting alone can well exceed that sum, owners with several bridges may pool their funds and apply it to one structure. For example, if a county has three bridges open to vehicular traffic, it is eligible for 3 x $5,642, or $16,926. All of it may be spent on one vehicular bridge that biennium.

We have entered into agreements with Benton and Linn counties, and we anticipate including Lane County. Together these three counties represent 19 of the 28 bridges. The agreements total $107,200 or 68% of our program budget. At this time, no reimbursements have been issued.

Lottery Funds

House Bill 3075 set side $320,000 of lottery revenues for rehabilitation of all covered bridges. These revenues are distributed through the Executive Department's Economic Development Fund for state parks. $12,800, or 4% is retained for the Economic Development Department's administrative costs. The remaining $307,200 was available to all covered bridge owners. Under this program, projects started after January 1, 1989, may be retroactively funded. Rehabilitation includes inspection, maintenance and replacement of all components of the covered portion of the bridge.

Since some projects work on a shoestring budget, this program allows owners to consider donated materials, tools, equipment rental and professional services as a match. The dollar value of those items is combined with the amount of cash spent on the project and reimbursement is based on 50% of this sum. However, the reimbursement cannot exceed the actual cash spent. Requests for reimbursements can be submitted at any time during the project. By reinvesting interim reimbursements in the project and matching them with donations, owners with a small amount of cash are able to fund a substantial project.

In response to a survey, owners of 25 bridges expressed interest in participating in this program. Their total estimated project costs were $1.5 million. The anticipated requests for reimbursements exceeded $525,000 or 171% of the available funds. We currently have 5 signed agreements with bridge owners. Another 4 owners have agreements that are in the process of being signed. These 9 owners represent 14 bridges, and a total in grants of $244,500, which is 80% of the program's $307,200 funding. To date,

we have disbursed $25,800, and another $17,500 is expected to go out shortly

Lottery Shortfall

Since this program is based on lottery revenues, available funding is a variable. Last month the Economic Development Department indicated that we should anticipate a 30% shortfall in lottery revenues. This will reduce our programa funds from $307,200 to $215,000. If no new applications are accepted, the current 14 agreements totalling $244,500 will exceed the available funds by $29,500. To mitigate the problem, we anticipate using unclaimed highway funds to make up this lottery shortfall. These monies will be applied toward those bridges carrying vehicular traffic, freeing up lottery funds for the nonvehicular bridges.

Review

In review, 28 of Oregon's 52 covered bridges are eligible for $158,000 of Highway Funds. Currently 19 bridges are participating in the program with grants amounting to $107,200. The remaining $50,800 will be used to cover lottery shortfalls. All of our 52 covered bridges are eligible for lottery funds. We received responses for 25 bridges, but due to the limited funding, around 14 are expected to participate at this time. These 14 bridges represent grant amounts of $244,500. We anticipate disbursing $215,000 in lottery proceeds. This $29,500 shortfall will be covered by unclaimed highway funds. Any remaining monies will be used to fund additional projects.

25 of our covered bridges will not receive any financial assistance this biennium. Based on survey response and estimated rehabilitation costs listed in the 1987 Covered Bridge Study, these bridges represent over $714,000 of needed work. Of the 12 bridges listed in the study as being in poor condition, 10 will still need attention.

Oregon Historical Markers
and
Covered Bridge Signing

During the 1989 Legislature, the Joint Committee on Ways and Means asked that a program be developed for historical markers and covered bridge signing. Ten thousand dollars was set aside for a study and progress report. There is a growing inventory of highway signs, accompanied by rapidly growing material and maintenance costs, that we are faced with how to finance. The study recommendations, and the allocations of available funding to historic markers and covered bridge signing, were developed by the diversely represented committee . . .

The consensus of the Committee was to separate those interested in historic markers and those in covered bridges into two subcommittees and to report back to a main committee composed of representative members of each group. The Committee recommends that of the $10,000 set aside by the Legislative Ways and Means Committee, $6,000 be used for covered bridges and $4,000 for historical markers. It is suggested that the covered bridge funds be used first to complete covered bridge identifier signing.

Covered Bridges Subcommittee

The Covered Bridge Subcommittee worked to update needs for signing and publicity to stimulate interest in the Oregon covered bridges. Linn and Lane Counties have clusters of covered bridges while some, such as Lincoln County, have bridges in scattered locations. The Subcommittee reached consensus on the following suggestions:

- two sets of criteria; one for single bridges and the other for clusters of bridges.
- Two types of signing; signing at the bridge and directional signing to the bridge(s).
- signing for a bridge reuires that the bridge not be too far from the highway and that road access must be in reasonably good condition (e.g., not gravel, unimproved, etc.)
- follow-up signing may be required on local roads and streets.
- do not sign for bridges more than 10 miles off a highway, especially for a single bridge location.

Two boys on bikes going home from school. Grave Creek Bridge, Josephine County.

- develop maps or brochures for individual bridges, being sure to coordinate with county and local jurisdictions.
- a site sign should photograph well.

A total amount of $2,000-3,000 was estimated for coverage at all fourteen Travel Information gazebos, depending up the artwork selected.
Priorities for completing Covered Bridge Signing:

1.	Complete task for furnishing each bridge with a sign that identifies it by name, the stream crossed, and the date built (33 bridges need signs).	$ 7,920
2.	Tour route signing - Linn County.	$ 3,300
3.	Tour route signing - Lane County.	$ 4,800
4.	Heritage Markers located at bridge locations having turnouts and parking areas.	$52,000
		$68,020

Publisher's note: In the November 1990 General Election, a measure aimed at properpty tax limitation was passed by the voters. All state funding will be hurt including monies usually allocated to Department of Transportation (highway funds), Parks Department and others. As there has been a decline in participation by the public in playing the state lottery, a "shortfall," noted in the report has already caused concern among committees working on local bridge restoration projects.

143

Glossary

Abutment — An abutment supports the end of a single or multi-span structure and, in general, supports the approach embankment. Usually of rock, concrete or timber, *see also:* Piling.

Approach — The passageway from the roadbed onto the bridge. Often of wood in older bridges, now concrete or asphalt.

Bridge — A structure that allows continuous passage over water, road or valley. Generally carries a path, road or railroad, but may also carry power lines or pipe lines. An observer quipped that since highways are not pretty to look at and bridges are, the only reason for highways is to connect the bridges.

Buttress — An abutting pier that braces a wall.

Ca. — *Circa,* an estimated date.

Chord — A main horizontal member of a truss. Traditional covered bridges often have upper and lower chords.

Covered bridge — A structure (*see:* Bridge), usually timber but recently a few are being built on bases of salvaged railroad flat cars, with a roof and usually siding as protection from weather.

Daylighting — Provision in design of covered bridges for allowing light to enter the closed bridge by various designs or sizes of windows.

Dead load — Weight of a bridge — gross weight.

Deck — The roadway surface of a bridge.

Diagonal — The timber affixed on an angle that connects upper and lower chords.

End post — A diagonal installed at either end of a truss.

Flying buttress — *(Arc-boutant)* A prop that arises from a support and ends against another part of a structure to provide added strength to the structure. In slang, sometimes called "out-riggers."

Foundation — The abutment that supports ends of a bridge. *See also:* Abutment.

Hewn timber — Finished surface of log shaped by hand tools applied here primarily in shaping a log into a truss.

Lower chord — The lower truss, also called stringer or girder in covered bridges.

National Register — The *National Register of Historic Places* is a list (in book form) maintained by the National Park Service of the nation's cultural resources deemed worthy of preservation. The list includes districts, archeological and historical sites, buildings, structures (including covered bridges) and selected objects of national, state and local worthiness.

ODOT — Oregon Department of Transportation.

Pier — A structure intended to support the ends of the spans of a multi-span superstructure at an intermediate location between abutments. *See also:* Abutment.

Piling — Logs (poles) driven into the ground on which a bridge or approach is mounted.

Pony truss — A low through truss that has no overhead or enclosing truss work. The word "pony" means something smaller than standard.

Portal — Entrance to a bridge, especially a through truss or arch.

Portal message — A plaque mounted above the entrance portal of a bridge on which indicia about the bridge, possibly the name of the bridge, has been affixed.

Portal weatherboard — Wood cover affixed inside a portal intended to shield lower truss and its joints from water splattered on wet days by vehicles.

Rafter — Any of the parallel beams that support a roof. In covered bridges, rafters form the peak in center of roof, the opposite ends resting on the top truss.

Span — Distance between abutments; the deck, if the deck is separate from approaches.

Spandrel — The area between the exterior curves of an arch and the roadway.

Stringer — Supporting timber under bridge deck.

Sway brace	*See:* Flying buttress.
Tie rod	Metal tension rods used in vertical position holding upper and lower chords in correct positions. These rods are threaded and can be adjusted if need be. Queenpost and Howe trusses use tension (tie) rods.
Through	Form of bridge in which traffic moves through the framework of a bridge.
Truss	A bridge with a framework of members, forming a triangle or system of triangles to support the weight of the bridge as well as passing loads.
Tuning tie rods	Periodic adjustment of tie rods (tension rods) to maintain specified tension between upper and lower trusses.
Upper chord	The upper truss, also called stringer or girder in covered bridges.

Bibliography

Books

Adams, Kramer A., *Covered Bridges of the West.* Howell-North. 1963.

Cockrell, Bill and Nick Cockrell. *Roofs Over Rivers.* Touchstone. 1978.

_____. *The New Guide to Oregon's Covered Bridges.* Oregon Sentinel. 1989.

Helsel, Bill. *World Guide to Covered Bridges.* The National Society for the Preservation of Covered Bridges. 1989.

Irving, Washington. *The Legend of Sleepy Hollow.* Morrow. 1987.

Lane, Oscar F. *World Guide to Covered Bridges.* The National Society for the Preservation of Covered Bridges. 1972.

Nelson, Lee H. *A Century of Oregon Covered Bridges 1851-1952.* Oregon Historical Society. 1976.

Smith, Dwight A., James B. Norman and Pieter T. Dykman. *Historic Highway Bridges of Oregon.* Oregon Historical Society. 1989.

Sloan, Eric. *American Barns and Covered Bridges.* Funk. 1954.

Periodicals

Ellsworth, Christine. "1990 Oregon Safari" in *Covered Bridge Topics.* Vol. XLVIII. No. 4. The National Society for the Preservation of Covered Bridges. Fall 1990.

McCoy, Imogene W. "Charming Americana Covered Bridge Spans Canal Over Original Water Right in Central Oregon" in *Covered Bridge Topics.* Apr. 8, 1968

"Touring Covered Bridge Country South of Eugene [Ore.]" in *Sunset Magazine.* Sep. 1990.

Special Studies

Hoffstetter, Dwayne. *Survey of Oregon's Historical Markers and Covered Bridge Signing.* Oregon State Transportation Committee. Sep. 11, 1990.

"Index of Covered Bridges in Oregon — 1947" in Planning Survey, Oregon State Highway Department, Traffic Engineering Division. Aug. 5, 1948.

Nagel, Carl Scott. "Historical-Geographical Analysis of Covered Bridges in Oregon" (thesis). Graduate College of Bowling Green State University. 1978.

Norman, James. *Oregon Covered Bridges; A Study for the 1989-1990 Legislature.* Oregon State Department of Transportation. 1988.

Richards, Carl P. *Covered Bridges in Oregon.* Oregon State Highway Commission. 1952.

Yih, Mae (Senator). *Concepts For A New Covered Bridge Bill [Covered Bridge Restoration and Preservation Programs].* Oregon Senate Interim Committee. Sep. 11, 1990.

Newspapers

"Army Reserves Destroy Historic Covered Bridge," in *Oregonian* (Portland). Oct. 5, 1955 p.19.

"A Covered Bridge Falls," in *Oregonian*. Feb. 3, 1943 p.8.

Campbell, Mary Ann. "Bridges to the Past" in Medford *Mail-Tribune*. Sep. 11, 1983.

Campbell, Mary Ann. "Time's Taking its Toll of Covered Bridges, the Roofs Over Rivers" in Medford *Mail-Tribune*. Jan. 4, 1979.

"Covered Bridge Felled by Snow," in *Capitol Journal* (Salem). Feb. 3, 1969.

"Covered Bridge To Give E. County 'Needed Amenity,' " in *Oregon Journal* (Portland). Oct. 10, 1981 p.5.

County's Only Covered Bridge Spans Grave Creek At Site Of Girl's Grave," in *Daily-Courier* (Grants Pass). Apr. 2, 1960 p.5.

Gardner, Fran. "County Demolishes One of Few Covered Bridges Still Remaining" in *Daily Tidings* (Ashland). Apr. 4, 1974.

Lampman, Linda. "The Covered Bridges Spanning Oregon's Past," in *Northwest Magazine* [Oregonian]. June 17, 1983.

"Linn Covets Doomed Covered Bridges," in *Oregon Statesman* (Salem). Jul. 9, 1972 p.1.

"Old Knights Bridge Just a Memory" in *Enterprise-Courier* (Oregon City). Aug.3, 1954.

"On the Road to Yesterday — [Any Person Riding or Driving Faster Than A Walk Upon This Bridge is Liable to a Fine of $100]" in *Oregon Journal* (Portland). Nov. 28, 1937.

"Over Johnson Creek — County to Construct Covered Bridge," in *Oregonian*. Sep. 30, 1981 p.B1.

"Peedee Kids Save Historic Polk Covered Bridge," in *Oregon Journal*. May 20, 1976 p.17.

"Polk Covered Bridge To Go; One Remains," in *Oregon Statesman*. May 31, 1962 Sec. 2, p.9.

"Put Linn's Museum in a Covered Bridge," in *Capitol Journal*. Aug. 27, 1962 Sec. 1, p.4.

"State is Planning to Move Bridge at Ritner Creek," in *Oregon Statesman*. Mar. 19, 1974 Sec. 2, p.9.

Thoele, Mike, "Aging Bridge Restructured," in *Register-Guard*. Jun. 1, 1989.

_____. "Bridging the Gap Between Old, New" in *Post-Intelligencer*. Jul. 16, 1989.

Vroman, Bob. "Hartmans Built County's Early-Day Bridges" in Medford *Mail-Tribune*. Jul. 19, 1959.

Webber, Bert. "Covered Bridge Loss Draws Blast By State Historians" in *Oregon Journal*. Apr. 6, 1974.

Index of Oregon Counties by County Number

01	Baker	19	Lake*
02	Benton*	20	Lane*
03	Clackamas*	21	Lincoln
04	Clatsop	22	Linn*
05	Columbia	23	Malheur
06	Coos*	24	Marion*
07	Crook	25	Morrow
08	Curry	26	Multnomah
09	Deschutes*	27	Polk*
10	Douglas*	28	Sherman
11	Gilliam*	29	Tillamook
12	Grant	30	Umatilla
13	Harney	31	Union
14	Hood River	32	Wallowa
15	Jackson*	33	Wasco
16	Jefferson	34	Washington
17	Josephine*	35	Wheeler
18	Klamath	36	Yamhill

* Has at least one covered bridge standing

Index of Oregon Covered Bridges
by County
with *World Guide* Numbers

Index of *Standing* Oregon Covered Bridges
By Map Location Number, Name, County

Early Day Bridge Builders — Fixers

On September 7, 1977, retired bridge construction experts Wesley and Lyal Hartman compiled a list of 27 covered bridges in Jackson County they either built from scratch or worked on. (• denotes photographs in this book)

3 along Thompson Creek
1 at town of Applegate on Applegate River
1 over Little Applegate River at confluence with Applegate River
1 over Yale Creek at Little Applegate River
1 over Beaver Creek at Applegate River
1 McKee Bridge over Applegate River •
1 at Del Rio (Rock Point) over Rogue River •
1 over Ward Creek in town of Rogue River
3 over Evans Creek:
    1 Minthorn Bridge •
    2 bridges at Wimer •
1 on East Fork Evans Creek at Milland Ranch
1 Laurelhurst (Peyton) over Rogue River •
1 over Big Butte Creek at town of Butte Falls
1 over Little Butte Creek at Brown Barrow
1 over Long Branch Creek
1 over Little Butte Creek at Lake Creek (village) store
1 over Lost Creek •
1 over Little Butte Creek at Will Heights
1 over Little Butte Creek in town of Eagle Point
1 over Antelope Creek •
1 over Yankee Creek •
1 over Little Butte Creek at Agate Road
1 over Bear Creek at Eagle Mills Jackson Hot Springs
1 Cameron Bridge (longest in county, 84-feet over Applegate River

Map continues on p.150

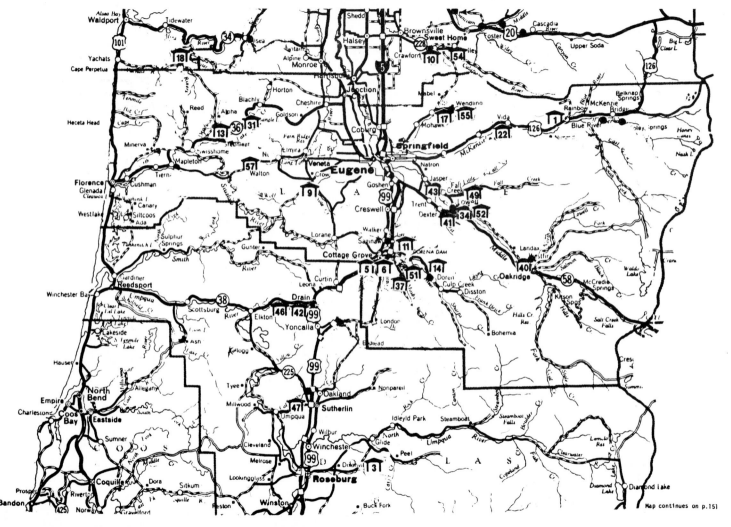

Map continues on p.151

150

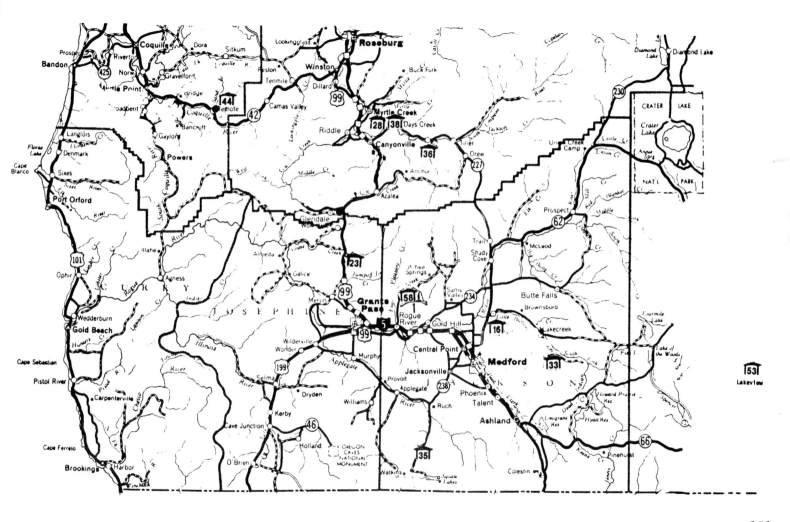

151

About the Authors

BERT WEBBER first encountered an Oregon covered bridge while riding in a Greyhound bus on a wintery day in 1941 when on a trip from San Francisco to Camp Clatsop on the Oregon coast. That bridge crossed Grave Creek in Josephine County.

In the following decades he has photographed many dozens of covered bridges, mainly with 4 x 5-inch Speed Graphic and later with 35mm cameras. Some of these pictures are included here in complement to the bridge portraits by John Snook.

Bert Webber, as a research-photojournalist, has authored or contributed to about 30 books (so far) all about some aspect of the Oregon country. He holds a Bachelor's degree with emphasis in jour-nalism from Whitworth College, and he earned the Master of Library Science degree from study at Portland State University and University of Portland. He was a school librarian for a number of years as well as owner of retail and wholesale businesses. He has always done some writing but turned to full-time writing when he left librarianship in 1970.

His aim is to write in language easily understood by the public but with authority so his books can be used by reference librarians.

Bert Webber is a member of the Covered Bridge Society of Oregon and of the National Society For The Preservation of Covered Bridges, headquartered in New England.

MARGIE WEBBER is a retired Registered Nurse who earned her baccalaureate degree in Nursing from the University of Washington. She is a fourth-generation photo lab assistant and for this book serves as Senior Editor. She often makes photographs which are included in the couple's books.

The Webber's make their home in Oregon's Rogue River Valley where there are half-a-dozen covered bridges within a few minutes drive. They have four grown children and are happily, at present, grandparents of seven grandchildren.

Illustration Credits

All of the John Snook photos and many of the other photos have not been previously published

Index

Page numbers in *italic* are illustrations

Notes

Notes

Notes

Notes

Notes